Enoch Rising

ENMEDURANKI, THE FALLEN WATCHERS, AND
THE KEY TO UNLOCKING EARLY
CHRISTIANITY

Juan Marcos Bejarano Gutierrez

Yaron Publishing
GRAND PRAIRIE, TEXAS

Copyright © 2018 by Juan Marcos Bejarano Gutierrez

All rights reserved. No part of this publication may be reproduced, distributed or transmitted in any form or by any means, including photocopying, recording, or other electronic or mechanical methods, without the prior written permission of the publisher, except in the case of brief quotations embodied in critical reviews and certain other noncommercial uses permitted by copyright law. For permission requests, write to the publisher, addressed "Attention: Permissions Coordinator," at the address below.

Juan Marcos Bejarano Gutierrez /Yaron Publishing
701 Forest Park Place
Grand Prairie, Texas 75052
www.CryptoJewishEducation.com

Book Layout ©2017 BookDesignTemplates.com

Ordering Information:
Quantity sales. Special discounts are available on quantity purchases by corporations, associations, and others. For details, contact the "Special Sales Department" at the address above.

Enoch Rising/ Juan Marcos Bejarano Gutierrez. —1st ed.
ISBN 9781791902254

Contents

Introduction 6
The Book of Enoch, 2 Enoch, and Sefer Hekhalot 13
The Biblical References 19
    Enoch's Walk with God 24
Enmenduranki and Mesopotamian Lore 27
    The Meaning of Metatron 36
    Enoch as Metatron 40
Enoch the Seer 43
Enoch the Scribe 61
Enoch the Priest 71
Enoch and the Prince of the Presence 83
Enoch as the Prince of the World 91
Enoch as the Lesser Deity 95
Enoch as Mediator 111
    Enoch as a Witness of God's Judgment 126
Enoch as a Messianic Figure 129
    Enoch as the Son of Man 135
    The Chosen and Anointed One 141
Enoch and the Angels 155
The Rise of Enochic Judaism 178
    Rabbinic Approaches to Enoch 196

Philo of Alexandria on Enoch... 199

　　The Targumim on Enoch.. 201

Enoch and the New Testament 205

　　The Significance of Enoch 207

Bibliography 216

Index... 235

To those searching for truth

"We naturally like what we have been accustomed to, and are attracted towards it. [...] The same is the case with those opinions of man to which he has been accustomed from his youth; he likes them, defends them, and shuns the opposite views."

— *Maimonides, The Guide for the Perplexed*

Introduction

Any person with only a rudimentary knowledge of the Hebrew Bible is undoubtedly acquainted with Adam, Abraham, and Moses. The individual with even a superficial familiarity with the New Testament has undoubtedly heard about Jesus, Peter, and Paul. *Enoch*, on the other hand, is a much less known biblical figure.

Three people bear the name Enoch in the Hebrew Bible.[1] The Enoch we are interested in appears only twice in the Hebrew Bible or what Christians refer to as the Old Testament.[2] He is referred to three times in the New Testament.[3] Given the lack of references, it would seem natural to believe that his importance would be limited, especially when considering the countless names found in the Bible's many genealogical lists.

The significance of Enoch goes far beyond these scant references, however. Aside from Abraham, Moses, and Elijah in the Hebrew Bible, and Jesus and Paul in the

---

[1] See Genesis 4:17 for Enoch son of Cain; See Genesis 25:4 for Enoch son of Midian.
[2] Genesis 5:21-24; I Chronicles 1:3. See also the Wisdom of Sirach or Ecclesiasticus 44:16.
[3] Luke 3:37, Hebrews 11:5, Jude 1:14–15.

New Testament, the unlikely figure of Enoch, at least from a literary standpoint, is one of the most significant biblical figures.

Enoch is credited with books that impacted other religious works written during the Second Temple era (515 BCE – 70 CE) and may have even rivaled in importance those books that we now consider to comprise the Hebrew Bible.[4] Whether he wrote these books or not is not a concern to the historian or the curious individual. What is important is that this material had a tremendous impact on evolving Judaism and later Christianity.

The various books of Enoch may also shed light on the influence of earlier Mesopotamian texts and Greek myths on Biblical history or, at the very minimum, the awareness of biblical authors of their cultural and religious surroundings. Most importantly, perhaps, the books of Enoch also unlock some of the mysteries, which first appear in the Hebrew Bible and then are greatly amplified in the New Testament without any explanation. The Enoch tradition also reveals a link between Jewish apocalypticism[5] of the Second Temple Era and Jewish mysticism of the post-Temple era.

---

[4] Enoch is mentioned in a wide range of literature during the Second Temple era. This includes the Testaments of the Twelve Patriarchs, the Sibylline Oracles, Philo, Josephus, Pseudo-Philo, 2 Baruch, Life of Adam and Eve, the *Testament of Abraham* among other texts.

[5] Annette Yoshiko Reed summarizes previously commonly held assumptions about apocalypses. Reed states: "Prior to the discovery of the Dead Sea Scrolls, it was commonplace for

The books of Enoch relate the story of fallen angels, i.e., the *Fallen Watchers*, the birth of giants, and the origins of demons.[6] Enochic literature tells the story of a man translated into heaven and designated as the messianic *Son of Man*.[7] The latter term is used extensively in the New Testament by Jesus.

In subsequent Enochic works, Enoch is taken to heaven, where he is transformed into an angelic being. Enoch assumed various roles and titles, which ultimately include a heavenly scribe, an expert in Secrets, the Prince of the Divine Presence, a heavenly priest[8],

---

scholars of Second Temple Judaism to locate the production of all apocalypses in 'conventicles,' small groups of antiestablishment prophets or visionaries who cultivated secret wisdom, isolated from the community at large. Taking Daniel as the model for the genre as a whole, scholars speculated that powerlessness and persecution drove the composition of apocalypses...we can no longer assume that all apocalypses derive from disenfranchised groups in distress, however well this explanation fits the two apocalypses now in the Christian canon (Daniel; Revelation). Annette Yoshiko Reed, *Fallen Angels and the History of Judaism and Christianity* (Cambridge: Cambridge Press, 2004), 61-62.

[6] See in Kevin Sullivan, "The Watchers Traditions in *1 Enoch* 6-16: The Fall of Angels and the Rise of Demons," in Angela Kim Harkins, Kelley Coblentz Bautch, and John C. Endres, eds., *The Watchers in Jewish and Christian Traditions* (Minneapolis: Fortress Press, 2014), 91-103.

[7] See Acts 2:36; Hebrews 4:14-16.

[8] See Hebrews 4:14-16 for an interesting comparison.

and most surprisingly, even as a lesser YHWH, the four-letter name of God.[9]

Such designations are critical to understanding many aspects of the New Testament.[10] They are nevertheless part of the history of polyform Judaism which is demonstrated by the survival of these ideas, so often identified as Christian, in later Jewish mystical literature.[11] Books related to Enoch also reveal the complex relationships that continued to exist between Jews and Christians and the heretical groups that stretched between them. The *Book of Giants,* for example, found in Qumran was known from Manicheanism, a syncretistic combination of Jewish, Christian, and Zoroastrian elements. The Manichean version of this text is based on the Jewish version found in Cave 4 at Qumran. The complex relationship between faiths is found in the founder of

---

[9] Speaking about Enoch, James Vanderkam notes, "The apotheosis that he experiences in this text is truly remarkable, one that will be difficult to match in the ensuing tradition." James C. Vanderkam, *Enoch: A Man for All Generations* (Columbia: University of South Carolina, 1995), 135. See also Annette Yoshiko Reed, *Fallen Angels and the History of Judaism and Christianity* (Cambridge: Cambridge Press, 2004), 1.

[10] "The remarkable use of the fourth title, 'son of man,' in the Similitudes have peaked the interest of New Testament scholars, some of whom, as noted, find the Similitudes to be important background information or even a direct source of the Gospel's attribution of this title to Jesus." James C. Vanderkam, *Enoch: A Man for All Generations* (Columbia: University of South Carolina, 1995), 138.

[11] Daniel Boyarin, "Beyond Judaisms: Metatron and the Divine Polymorphy of Ancient Judaism," Journal for the Study of Judaism 41 (2010):323-365.

Manicheanism. Mani, who lived from 216-277 C.E., was a one-time member of the *Elchaisites*, a Jewish-Christian group often characterized as Gnostic and Mani's likely source of familiarization with the Enochic literature.[12]

Enoch did not merely represent an individual but ultimately a movement that embraced the mystical and, at times, may have even opposed what we so instinctively take for granted as normative Judaism and even early Christianity.[13] The literature ascribed to Enoch proved a challenge to Jews and Christians. Each group took seemingly complementary stances towards its legitimacy or dismissal at different times. Whatever the case, the Enoch tradition has survived. Whether it has done so by existing on the periphery or the margin of Jewish or

---

[12] James C. VanderKam, *Enoch: A Man for All Generations* (Columbia: University of South Carolina, 1995), 125. See also Andrei A. Orlov, *From Patriarch to the Youth: The Metatron Tradition in 2 Enoch,* PhD diss. (Milwaukee: Marquette University, 2004), 73.

[13] Regarding the complexity of Judaism, Daniel Boyarin states: "Where [Alan] Segal seems clearly to imagine an 'orthodox core' to Judaism that pre-exists and then develops into what would become rabbinism, I imagine a Judaism that consists of manifold historical developments of a polyform tradition in which no particular form has claim to either orthodoxy or centrality over others." Daniel Boyarin, "Beyond Judaisms: Metatron and the Divine Polymorphy of Ancient Judaism," Journal for the Study of Judaism 41 (2010):326.

Christian identity, it has endured.[14] The fascination surrounding it continues to flourish.

The intrigue and appeal surrounding Enoch are based upon a few verses which provide support for the view that Enoch circumvented death and instead was taken alive into God's presence. This places Enoch in the same league as Elijah. Perhaps Moses, in certain traditions, as the only individuals to have entered God's presence alive. Enoch and Elijah are the only biblical figures to have escaped death, thus adding to the mystique and intrigue.[15]

---

[14] Annette Yoshiko Reed notes that after the rejection of the Enochic tradition by Church fathers like Augustine, Enochic literature was largely lost to the West. Reed states: "To an even greater degree than in ages past, the mystery surrounding Enoch came to be associated with lost books and secret scrolls, wisdom suppressed and writings forgotten. Even as the books themselves were gone, the ancient allusions remained. It could not have escaped the attention of Christian Kabbalists that early Christian literature and Jewish mystical texts like the Zohar both mentioned…Pico della Mirandola (1463-1494) even professed to have bought such a book at a very high price, to the amusement of his more skeptical colleague, Johannes Reuchlin (1455-1522)." Annette Yoshiko Reed, *Fallen Angels and the History of Judaism and Christianity* (Cambridge: Cambridge Press, 2004), 2.

[15] The *Book of Jubilees* 7:38-39 provides a unique record to the contrary.

CHAPTER 1

The Book of Enoch, 2 Enoch, and Sefer Hekhalot

While many books contain references to Enoch, three works are focused explicitly on Enoch. The first is the Book of Enoch, or I Enoch.[1] The second is 2 Enoch, or Slavonic Enoch because it is only preserved in the Slavonic language. The last is *Sefer Hekhalot*, i.e., the Book of Palaces. *Sefer Hekhalot* is also referred to as 3 Enoch.

The first book of Enoch is a composite work. It consists of five initially independent texts.[2] These include

---

[1] I Enoch is preserved in its entirety only in Ethiopic. However, Aramaic fragments were found at Qumran. See Jazef. T. Milik, ed., *The Books of Enoch: Aramaic Fragments of Qumran Cave 4* (Oxford: Oxford, 1976).

[2] Annette Yoshiko Reed, *Fallen Angels and the History of Judaism and Christianity* (Cambridge: Cambridge Press, 2004), 3. For discussion on the Ethiopic text of the first book of Enoch and its relationship to other manuscripts, see pgs. 17-20. See also John

the *Book of the Watchers* (Chapters 1-36)³; the *Book of Parables* or the *Book of Similitudes* (Chapters 37-71); the *Astronomical Treatise* (Chapters 72-82); the *Book of Dream Visions* (Chapters 83-90)⁴; and the *Letter of Enoch* to his children (Chapters 91-107).⁵

J. Collins, *The Apocalyptic Imagination: An Introduction to Jewish Apocalyptic Literature* (Grand Rapids: Wm. B. Eerdmans Publishing Co., 1998), 43

³ Annette Yoshiko Reed believes the redactional process for the Book of Watchers took place during Alexander the Great's conquest of Judea and the wars of succession that followed. Ibid., 59.

⁴ James Vanderkam identifies a subsection of the Book of Dream Visions as the Animal Apocalypse. This consists of I Enoch 85-90. James C. VanderKam, *Enoch: A Man for All Generations* (Columbia: University of South Carolina, 1995), 70. Annette Yoshiko Reed states: "The Book of Dreams and Epistle of Enoch provide important evidence for the reinterpretation of the Book of the Watchers and its account of angelic descent to fit the needs of a new age. Nevertheless, their differences demonstrate the dangers of reading I Enoch as a single document without some sensitivity to the evolving nature of the Enochic literary tradition and the progressive reinterpretation of Enoch and his role as an antediluvian revealer of heavenly secrets. Annette Yoshiko Reed, *Fallen Angels and the History of Judaism and Christianity* (Cambridge: Cambridge Press, 2004), 61.

⁵ J. R. Porter, *The Lost Bible: Forgotten Scriptures Revealed* (New York: Shelter Harbor Press, 2010), 30. See also George W.E. Nickelsburg and James C. Vanderkam, *1 Enoch: The Hermeneia Translation* (Minneapolis: Fortress Press, 2012), 1-15. James Vanderkam also suggests that another section termed the Apocalypse of Weeks should be identified. According to Vanderkam, this section consists of I Enoch 93:1-10 and 91:11-17. See

A key feature of I Enoch is that while a Messiah is mentioned, a Davidic style Messiah is absent. Nevertheless, it introduces a figure which strongly echoes some passages in the New Testament. The First Book of Enoch, or at least parts of it, was likely written as early as the end of the 3rd century BCE.

2 Enoch and *Sefer Hekhalot* are subsequent renditions of the Enoch story with significant differences. Speculation on the date of composition of either text varies greatly. 2 Enoch was likely written before the destruction of the Second Temple in 70 CE. 2 Enoch is often thought of as a potentially Christian text. In comparison, 3 Enoch is a rabbinic text following the pattern of the mystical ascent literature known as the *Hekhalot*.[6]

Francis Andersen provides the following assessment of 2 Enoch:

> "In every respect 2 Enoch remains an enigma. So long as the date and location remain unknown, no use can be made of it for historical purposes. The present writer is inclined to place the book – or at least its original nucleus-early rather than late; and in a Jewish rather than in a Christian community. But by the very marginal if not deviant

---

also James C. VanderKam, *Enoch: A Man for All Generations* (Columbia: University of South Carolina, 1995), 63.

[6] Despite its origins in Jewish mystical circles, Annette Yoshiko Reed suggests that the allusions to the Book of Watchers within *Sefer Hekhalot* reflect Christian influence. Annette Yoshiko Reed, *Fallen Angels and the History of Judaism and Christianity* (Cambridge: Cambridge Press, 2004), 16.

character of their beliefs, its users could have been Gentile converts to moral monotheism based on belief in the antediluvian God of the Bible as Creator, but not as the God of Abraham or Moses."[7]

Despite this assessment, 2 Enoch appears to form the bridge between 1 Enoch and 3 Enoch as far as the development of titles and roles assigned to Enoch is concerned. The inclusion in 2 Enoch of ideas that seem to post-date the Second Temple era has raised some questions. To this, Andrei Orlov opines that,

"The presence of these seemingly late concepts in the Second Temple Jewish text understandably raises many questions about the provenance of the pseudepigraphon and even leads some scholars to believe that these developments might represent later interpolations which the Slavonic text has acquired during its long transmission history in the Greek and Slavonic mileux. A close textual analysis, however, reveals the early premishnaic mold of the hero's roles and titles and their connection with the early apocalyptic imagery found in the Slavonic apocalypse;"[8]

---

[7] James C. VanderKam, *Enoch: A Man for All Generations* (Columbia: University of South Carolina, 1995), 158.

[8] Andrei A. Orlov, *From Patriarch to the Youth: The Metatron Tradition in 2 Enoch,* PhD diss. (Milwaukee: Marquette University, 2004), 204.

Regarding *Sefer Hekhalot* or 3 Enoch, the word *Hekhalot* refers to a mystical ascent into heavenly palaces and finally into God's presence.

Another variation on Enoch's exalted status is evident through the view that he was transformed into an angelic being and subsequently placed as head of God's court.[9] This view is only attested to in 3 Enoch, which some scholars regard as having been written in the fifth century. 3 Enoch relates the ascent of Rabbi Ishmael to heaven. This text centers on the exchange of Enoch's earthly clothing to "anoint him with my delightful oil and put him into the clothes of my glory."[10]

---

[9] Moshe Idel notes Enoch's unique experience. "Enoch is the only living person for whom…luminous garments, reminiscent of Adam's lost garments of light, were made." Moshe Idel, "Enoch is Metatron," Immanuel 24/25 (1990): 224. *Pirke de Rabbi Eliezer* 14 states: "What was Adam's garment [before his sin]: A fragrant mist of onycha and a divine aura of glory covered him. After he ate the fruit of the tree, the onycha's mist was divested from him, the aura of glory departed from him, and he saw himself naked."

[10] Larry W. Hurtado, *One God, One Lord* (Minneapolis: Fortress Press, 1988), 53. See also Chapter VII Metatron in Joseph Dan, *The Ancient Jewish Mysticism* (Tel Aviv, MOD Books, 1993), 108-124; Daniel Abrahams, "The Boundaries of Divine Ontology: The Inclusion and Exclusion of Metatron in the Godhead," HTR 87 (1994): 291-321; Andrei A. Orlov, "Titles of Enoch-Metatron in 2 Enoch," Journal for the Study of the Pseudepigrapha 18 (1998): 71-86; Andrei A. Orlov, *The Enoch-Metatron Tradition* (Tübingen: Mohr Siebeck, 2005).

CHAPTER 2

The Biblical References

The brief reference to Enoch in Genesis possibly betrays the strong Mesopotamian influence on the biblical author(s) and a connection to another obscure Biblical passage regarding the mythic rise of the *Nephilim*.[1] At the very least, it shows the authors of Genesis were undoubtedly aware of their cultural and theological milieu. Enoch's elevated status among many Jews of the Second Temple period, the rise of Enochic Judaism, and the rabbinic preservation of views supporting and opposing popular views of Enoch reveal the flowering of diverse Biblical interpretations and a

---

[1] Genesis 6:4. John J. Collins opines the following: "the Enochic movement...originated in the confrontation with Mesopotamian culture in the eastern Diaspora and its 'scientific' interests developed in that setting. The subsequent development of an eschatologically oriented apocalyptic movement seems to have prompted by the culture crisis of the Hellenistic age, well in advance of the Antiochian persecution." J.J. Collins, *Seers, Sybils, and Sages in Hellenistic-Roman Judaism SJSJ 54* (Leiden: Brill, 1997), 51-52.

source of tension in emerging Jewish Aggadic literature regarding this heroic figure.[2]

Out of all the Enoch traditions, Genesis 5 appears to hold claim as the oldest Enoch passage.[3] Enoch first appears in the genealogy of Adam in Genesis 5. Genesis 5:19-24 states:

> "And Jared lived a hundred sixty and two years, and begot Enoch. And Jared lived after he begot Enoch eight hundred years, and begot sons and daughters.²⁰ And all the days of Jared were nine hundred sixty and two years; and he died.²¹ And Enoch lived sixty and five years, and begot Methuselah.²² And Enoch walked with God after he begot Methuselah three hundred years, and begot sons and daughters.²³ And all the days of Enoch were three hundred sixty and five years.²⁴ *And Enoch walked with God, and he was not; for God took him.*"

The genealogies of Genesis follow a standard pattern. In the Genesis list of chapter 5, the following formula is used: "Person A" becomes the father of "Person B," "Person B" becomes the father of "Person C." Any deviation from this format is used to highlight the individual in question.[4] Several examples of this are available, including the genealogy's reference to Adam who

---

[2] Aggadah refers to non-legal exegetical texts preserved in the Talmud and Midrashim.

[3] James C. VanderKam, *Enoch: A Man for All Generations* (Columbia: University of South Carolina, 1995), 13.

[4] Ibid., 4-5.

"begot a son in his own likeness, after his image; and called his name Seth" and the birth of Noah to Lamech, in Genesis 5:29,

> "And he [Lamech] called his name Noah, saying: 'This same shall comfort us in our work and in the toil of our hands, which cometh from the ground which the Lord hath cursed.'"

Some differences are immediately apparent between Enoch's life and the other individuals mentioned in the genealogy of Genesis 5. Enoch appears as the *seventh generation* from Adam. He is 65 years old at his first son's birth, which incidentally ties with Mahalalel for the lowest in the genealogy. The most obvious difference, however, is his shortened lifespan and, of course, the somewhat cryptic statement in verse 24 stating as is traditionally rendered that,

> "Enoch walked with God, and he was not; for God took him."

Enoch's life's brevity is further accentuated because he lies between the two longest-living individuals included in the list - Jared, who lived to be 962 years, and between his son Methuselah who died at the age of 969 years.[5] These differences lead the reader to question the significance of Enoch as the seventh in the list, the importance of his lifespan of 365 years, and most importantly, what is meant by the phrase,

---

[5] Ibid., 4.

וַיִּתְהַלֵּךְ חֲנוֹךְ, אֶת-הָאֱלֹהִים; וְאֵינֶנּוּ, כִּי-לָקַח אֹתוֹ אֱלֹהִים.

The meaning of the phrase is more complicated than it may first appear. What does the Biblical author mean by *v'yithalech,* for example?[6] The most often used translation is to *go, come, or walk.* An alternate rendering, i.e., *depart,* or *go away,* is also possible. The second area of interest is what exactly is meant by *et haElohim.*[7] The term *elohim* is most often refers to God. Yet, as is well known, it may also refer to rulers, judges, and most interestingly to other heavenly powers, e.g., gods, angels, etc. The last possibility is an issue which will be discussed shortly.

The meaning of Enoch's name is also debatable. Genesis 4:17 relates that Cain's wife gave birth to a son named Enoch. Cain built a city which he named after him. One possibility suggested by James Vanderkam is that the author of the text may have desired to connect Enoch's name to the Hebrew word for dedication, *chanukah.*[8]

---

[6] Go, come, walk. Dr. Richard Whitaker, *Revised Brown-Driver-Briggs Hebrew-English Lexicon,* 1995.

[7] Plural in number: a. rulers, judges, either as divine representatives at sacred places or as reflecting divine majesty and power. b. divine ones, superhuman beings including God and angels. Dr. Richard Whitaker, *Revised Brown-Driver-Briggs Hebrew-English Lexicon,* 1995.

[8] James C. VanderKam, *Enoch: A Man for All Generations,* (Columbia: University of South Carolina, 1995), 12. Dedication, consecration. Dr. Richard Whitaker, *Revised Brown-Driver-*

W.F. Albright suggested that Enoch or *Hanoch* may also be connected to the Hebrew word *Hanich* meaning "retainer or vassal."[9] While this view is not definitive, Genesis 14:14 provides some evidence to buttress this possibility. In this passage, Abram leads a mission to rescue his nephew Lot, who had been captured during a conflict of various Canaanite kings. The text states that Abram,

> "led forth his trained men (*et hanichav*), born in his house, three hundred and eighteen, and pursued as far as Dan."[10]

Either of these possible meanings justifies the view that Enoch's name serves to underscore his relationship with God. If Enoch is related to *Chanukah*, then Enoch is dedicated to God; if Enoch is related to *Hanich*, then

---

Briggs Hebrew-English Lexicon, 1995. See Deuteronomy 20:5; I Kings 8:63; 2 Chronicles 7:5.

[9] W.F. Albright, "The Babylonian matter in the PreDeuteronomic Primeval History [JE] in Genesis 1-11," Journal of Biblical Literature 58 [1939]. A less accepted view regarding the meaning of Enoch's name is put forth by P. Grelot who argued that the intended meaning of Enoch is related to wisdom and understanding. Grelot is dependent however on Arabic and Ethiopic cognates to support his view, though later descriptions of Enoch certainly include the reception and transmission of divine knowledge along the lines of Enmenduranki. P. Grelot, "The Legend of Enoch according to the Apocrypha and the Bible: Origin and Significance", RSR 46 (1958):186.

[10] James C. VanderKam, *Enoch: A Man for All Generations*, (Columbia: University of South Carolina, 1995), 11.

Enoch is a retainer of God, always devoted to His service, a striking similarity to the Sumerian King Enmeduranki which will be discussed shortly. The word *Hanoch* may also be related to the word *Hinuch,* meaning instruction or initiation.[11]

Enoch's Walk with God

The next point of interest in Enoch's life and uniqueness is what the Biblical author seeks to convey when he states that "Enoch *walked with* God." In the Hebrew, Genesis 5:22 reads,

וַיִּתְהַלֵּךְ חֲנוֹךְ, אֶת-הָאֱלֹהִים; וְאֵינֶנּוּ, כִּי-לָקַח אֹתוֹ אֱלֹהִים.

and this phrase appears in only one other Biblical passage. Genesis 6:9 states,

אֶת-הָאֱלֹהִים, הִתְהַלֶּךְ-נֹחַ.

Noah walked with God. In reference to Noah, the Torah implies that he was a righteous man, blameless in his generation. The absence of this note, when describing Enoch, provided rabbis of later centuries with the latitude to question the general assumption of Enoch's righteousness. Nevertheless, the connotation of *v'yithalech* appears to support the view that Enoch's

---

[11] Ibid., 11. See Deuteronomy 20:5; I Kings 8:63; II Chronicles 7:5.

walk with God was unique among his peers and intimate in his relationship with God.[12]

Further investigation reveals that the author's depiction of Enoch's relationship with God was perhaps much more complicated than is first assumed. The Hebrew text of Genesis 5:22 states:

וַיִּתְהַלֵּךְ חֲנוֹךְ אֶת-הָאֱלֹהִים, אַחֲרֵי הוֹלִידוֹ אֶת-מְתוּשֶׁלַח

Here the Biblical author states that Enoch walked with *ha-Elohim* and includes the definite article, *ha*. In both instances in which the author says that Enoch walked with God, he uses the definite article, *ha*. Genesis 5:24 states that,

וַיִּתְהַלֵּךְ חֲנוֹךְ, אֶת-הָאֱלֹהִים

The reference to Enoch's disappearance in verse 24, (…then he was no more for God took him) does not include the definite article:

וְאֵינֶנּוּ, כִּי-לָקַח אֹתוֹ אֱלֹהִים.

While arguably a minor point, the absence of the definite article strengthens the famous rendering of *elohim*

---

[12] To further support this view, C. Westermann argued that I Samuel 25:15-16 may be used to interpret as a friendly every day interaction. "Yet the men were very good to us, and we suffered no harm, and we never missed anything when we were in the fields, as long as we were with them."

to mean angels instead of God in this context.[13] That possibility opened the doors to a complex view of Enoch's relationship with God and the *Benei ha'elohim* of Genesis 6, whose actions eventually led to the flood and became the source material for subsequent Enochic literature. The story of the Fallen Watchers will be addressed more fully in chapter twelve.

Each of the subsequent chapters will focus on the various titles and roles Enoch assumed. Each chapter will look at the development of these roles beginning with I Enoch and review the expansion of this concept in subsequent Enochic works.

---

[13] For a more extensive discussion on the terms *Benei Elohim, Benei Elim, Bar Elohin*, see Chris Seeman, "The Watchers Traditions and Gen 6:1-4 (MT and LXX)," in Angela Kim Harkins, Kelley Coblentz Bautch, and John C. Endres, eds., *The Watchers in Jewish and Christian Traditions* (Minneapolis: Fortress Press, 2014), 29.

CHAPTER 3

Enmenduranki and Mesopotamian Lore

Akkadian sources provide parallel stories to the Genesis account of creation, in the myth of *Enuma Elish,* and most strikingly to the biblical account of the Deluge, in the *Epic of Gilgamesh.*[1] Akkadian genealogical lists also serve both as a critical source of comparison and illumination for Enoch's story.[2] While Noah is typically compared to Utnapishtim in the *Epic of Gilgamesh*, in some sense, the Book of Enoch transfers the trek of Gilgamesh to Enoch, who was taken into heaven to learn secret knowledge about his descendant Noah, who in turn was destined to survive the coming flood.[3]

---

[1] The Akkadian Empire was the first Mesopotamian Empire. It was centered on the city of Akkad, somewhere in present day Iraq.

[2] James C. VanderKam, *Enoch: A Man for All Generations* (Columbia: University of South Carolina, 1995), 6.

[3] Ibid., 101.

Like the Biblical genealogy found in Genesis chapter 5, the Akkadian genealogical lists also emphasize the individuals' lifespan. The genealogy list of Genesis mentions a lifespan of up to 969 years. The Akkadian lists also include very long lifespans (regarding reigns), albeit ranging from 3,600 to 72,000 years. The "Sumerian antediluvian King" lists date from 1500 BCE to 165 BCE. Incidentally, the tenth individual in the Akkadian genealogical list is Utnapishtim, the hero of the flood paralleling Noah's placement in the Biblical list.[4]

However, of most significant interest to us is the individual who lies in the list's seventh place, like Enoch. That individual is Enmeduranki or Enmendurranna.[5] The city in which Enmeduranki reigned was the city of Sippar. Sippar was the city of the sun god. In Sumerian, the sun god was named Utu, and in Akkadian, his name was Shamash. Utu or Shamash was worshipped in the temple Ebabarra. The fact that Sippar was associated with the worship of the Sun is telling. A solar year is 365

---

[4] For more information on the Sumerian King List see S. Langdon, "The Chaldean Kings before the Flood," JRAS 42 (1923): 251-259.

[5] Andrei Orlov opines, "In my judgment, the Enmeduranki tradition provides a sharp illustration of the fact that the celestial roles of this Mesopotamian hero served as a decisive pattern for the future heavenly roles of his Jewish counterpart, the patriarch Enoch." Andrei A. Orlov, *From Patriarch to the Youth: The Metatron Tradition in 2 Enoch,* PhD diss. (Milwaukee: Marquette University, 2004), 32.

days long. Incidentally, Enoch's lifespan totaled 365 years.[6]

What is most relevant about Enmeduranki is his special connection to the divine world of the Mesopotamian pantheon.[7] Andrei Orlov relates the following:

> "In three copies of the List, he [Enmeduranki] occupies *the seventh place*, which in the Genesis genealogy belongs to Enoch. Moreover, in other Mesopotamian sources, Enmeduranki appears in many roles and situations which demonstrate remarkable similarities with Enoch's story."[8]

The Akkadian text, from the library of Ashurbanipal, reads as follows:

> "Shamash in Ebabarra [appointed] Enmeduranki [king of Sippar], the beloved of Anu, Enlil, [and Ea]. Shamash, and Adad [brought him in] to their assembly, Shamash and Adad [honored him],

---

[6] Andre Orlov points the work of James Vanderkam who argues that the, "author responsible for the biblical portrayal of Enoch in Gen 5:21-24 was aware of these broader Mesopotamian traditions which serve as a prototype for Enoch's figure, whose symbolical age of 365 years reflects the link between the patriarch and the solar cult of Shamash." Andrei A. Orlov, *From Patriarch to the Youth: The Metatron Tradition in 2 Enoch,* PhD diss. (Milwaukee: Marquette University, 2004), 33.

[7] James C. VanderKam, *Enoch: A Man for All Generations* (Columbia: University of South Carolina, 1995), 7.

[8] Andrei A. Orlov, *From Patriarch to the Youth: The Metatron Tradition in 2 Enoch,* PhD diss. (Milwaukee: Marquette University, 2004), 33.

Shamash and Adad [set him] on a large throne of gold, they showed him how to observe oil on water, a mystery of Anu [Enlil and Ea] they gave him, the tablets of the gods, the liver, a secret of heaven and [underworld], they put in his hand the cedar-rod, beloved of the great gods. (II. 1-9)" [9]

What is most important to us in this passage is the ascent of Enmenduranki to the assembly of the gods by Shamash and Adad. Consequently, the uniqueness of Enmenduranki's relationship with them. According to this passage, the gods provided Enmenduranki with knowledge of divination. Enmenduranki was tasked with relaying this to other humans. Enmenduranki is subsequently credited with the creation of a school of diviner-priests.[10]

Enmenduranki's ascendancy to the court of the gods is also referred to by Nebuchadnezzar I, who lived from 1124 -1103 BCE. Nebuchadnezzar I, the fourth king of the second dynasty of Isin, the fourth dynasty of Babylon, speaks of himself as follows:

"Distant scion of kingship, seed preserved from before the flood, Offspring of Enmenduranki's, king of Sippar, who set up the pure bowl and the

---

[9] Translation by W. Lambert, *"Enmenduranki and Related Matters"*, JCS 21 (1967): 126-38.
[10] James C. VanderKam, *Enoch: A Man for All Generations* (Columbia: University of South Carolina, 1995), 8.

cedar wood, Who sat in the presence of Shamash and Adad, the divine adjudicators."[11]

The text from Nineveh is exceptionally significant in understanding the roles of the seventh antediluvian hero. The text includes the functions that Enmeduranki fills as a consequence of his contact with humans and divine beings. Enmeduranki is described as a learned savant, a diviner, a priest, and a guardian of secrets. These roles are significant in understanding the offices that Enoch and the figure Metatron play in later Jewish tradition.[12]

Like Enmeduranki, the patriarch Enoch was skilled in the divination, received and interpreted mantic dreams, ascended into the heavenly court, and received divine secrets from angels and ultimately God himself. John J. Collins notes that like Enmeduranki,

"Enoch, too, is taken into the heavenly council and shown the tablets of heaven. While the Jewish text does not pick up the Babylonian methods of divination, Enoch corresponds to Enmeduranki

---

[11] Translation by W. Lambert, "*Enmenduranki and Related Matters*", JCS 21 (1967): 126-127.

[12] Andrei A. Orlov, *From Patriarch to the Youth: The Metatron Tradition in 2 Enoch,* PhD diss. (Milwaukee: Marquette University, 2004), 35. It is worth noting that the Enochic tradition is not the only source of influence for the various roles assumed by Metatron. Other exalted angels including Michael, Yahoel, Melchizedek, among others. Ibid., 115.

insofar as he is a primeval archetypal mediator of revelation."[13]

He returns to earth and shares it with his son and other people. 2 Enoch 33 relates that God revealed Enoch the importance of his writings. They were intended to distribute knowledge for the benefit of humankind.

> "2 And now, Enoch, all that I have told you, all that you have understood, all that you have seen of heavenly things, *all that you have seen on earth, and all that I have written in books by my great wisdom*, all these things I have devised and created from the uppermost foundation to the lower and to the end, and there is no counselor nor inheritor to my creations…
>
> 5 If I turn away my face, then all things will be destroyed.
>
> 6 And apply your mind, Enoch, and know him who is speaking to you, and take thence the books which you yourself have written…
>
> 9 Give them the books of the handwriting, and they will read (them) and will know me for the creator of all things, and will understand how there is no other God but me.

---

[13] John J. Collins, "The Sage in the Apocalyptic and Pseudepigraphic Literature," in *The Sage in Israel and the Ancient Near East*, ed. John G. Gammie (Warsaw: Eisenbrauns, 1990), 346.

10 *And let them distribute the books of your handwriting–children to children, generation to generation, nations to nations.*

11 And I will give you, Enoch, my intercessor, the archistratege Michael, for the handwritings of your fathers Adam, Seth, Enos, Cainan, Mahalaleel, and Jared, your father."[14]

2 Enoch 47 also states:

"1 And now, my children, lay thought on your hearts, mark well the words of your father, which are all (come) to you from the Lord's lips.

2 *Take these books of your father's handwriting and read them.*

3 For the books are many, and in them, you will learn all the Lord's works, all that has been from the beginning of creation, and will be till the end of time.

4 And if you will observe my handwriting, you will not sin against the Lord; because there is no other except the Lord, neither in heaven, nor in

---

[14] 2 Enoch 24:3 states "[Listen, Enoch, and pay attention to these worlds of mine!] For not even to my angels have I explained my secrets, not related to them their origin, nor my endlessness [and inconceivableness], as I devise the creatures, as I am making them known to you today…" Francis Andersen, "2 (Slavonic Apocalypse of) Enoch," in *The Old Testament Pseudepigrapha*, ed. J.H. Charlesworth (New York: Doubleday, 1985), 142.

earth, nor in the very lowest (places), nor in the (one) foundation."

3 Enoch develops the Enoch story in a radical direction. It relates that the patriarch Enoch was transformed into an angelic power titled Metatron and was seated on the LORD's throne. Incidentally, Andrei Orlov characterizes Metatron as God's secretary.[15] Crispin Fletcher-Louis noted that in contrast to later Enochic tradition, in the *Book of Watchers*,

> "Enoch has peculiar rights of access to the divine presence (chs. 14-15), however, he is not explicitly said to be divine or angelic."[16]

Sefer Hekhahot also states:

> "Rabbi Ishmael said: Metatron, the Prince of the Presence, said to me;
>
> (1) All these things, the Holy One, blessed be He, made for me: He made me a Throne, similar to the Throne of Glory. And He spread over me a curtain of splendor and brilliant appearance, of beauty, grace, and mercy, similar to the curtain of the Throne of Glory; and on it were fixed all kinds of lights in the universe.

---

[15] Andrei A. Orlov, *From Patriarch to the Youth: The Metatron Tradition in 2 Enoch,* PhD diss. (Milwaukee: Marquette University, 2004), 151.

[16] Crispin H.T. Fletcher-Louis, *All the Glory of Adam: Liturgical Anthropology in the Dead Sea Scrolls, Volume 42* (Boston: Brill, 2002), 21.

(2) And He placed it at the door of the Seventh Hall and seated me on it.

(3) And the herald went forth into every heaven, saying: This is Metatron, my servant. I have made him into a prince and a ruler over all the princes of my kingdoms and over all the children of heaven, except the eight great princes, the honored and revered ones who are called YHWH, by the name of their King.

(4) And every angel and every prince who has a word to speak in my presence (before me) shall go into his presence (before him) and shall speak to him (instead)."[17]

The transformation of Enoch into Metatron is without question a critical aspect of later Enochic lore. Crispin Fletcher-Louis comments that,

> "3 Enoch's account of the transformation of Enoch into the principal angel Metatron represents something of the climax of earlier Enoch traditions."[18]

The great scholar of Jewish mysticism, Gershom Scholem, commented on the different streams of development on Metatron tradition including other prominent angels in biblical or Jewish tradition. Scholem wrote,

---

[17] 3 Enoch 10:1-4.
[18] Crispin H. T. Fletcher-Louis, *Luke-Acts: Angels, Christology, and Soteriology* (Tubingen: Mohr-Seibeck, 1997), 156.

"One aspect identifies Metatron with Jahoel or Michael and knows nothing of his transfiguration from a human being into an angel. The Talmudic passages concerned with Metatron are of this type. The other aspect identifies Metatron with the figure of Enoch as he is depicted in apocalyptic literature, and permeated that aggadic and targumic literature which, although not necessarily of a later date than Talmud, was outside of it. When the Book of Hekhaloth or 3 Enoch was composed, the two aspects had already become intertwined."[19]

The Meaning of Metatron

There are many possible etymologies for the term Metatron. Philip Alexander speculates whether Metatron's name originated in mystical Hekhalot or Merkabah manuscripts and maybe an artificially constructed magical word.[20] Various scholars including Hugo Odeberg, Adolf Jellinek, and Marcus Jastrow suggested the name might have originated from either Mattara (מטרא), i.e.,

---

[19] Gershom G. Scholem, *Jewish Gnosticism, Merkabah Mysticism, and Talmudic Tradition* (New York: Jewish Theological Seminary of America, 1960), 51.

[20] Philip Alexander, "3 (Hebrew Apocalypse of) Enoch," in *The Old Testament Pseudepigrapha*, ed., J.H. Charlesworth (New York: Doubleday, 1985), 1.243.

keeper of the watch, or the verb Memater (ממטר) meaning to guard, or to protect.[21]

In the *Sefer* or *Sidrei Shimmusha Rabbah*, written in the medieval period, Enoch is clad in light. He is the protector or custodian of the souls ascending to heaven.[22] The name Metatron might be derived from the Persian name Mithras.[23] Hugo Odeberg noted various parallels between Mithras and Metatron based on their positions in heaven and duties.

Metatron could be comprised of two Greek words for *after* and *throne*, μετὰθρόνος (meta/thronos). Combining these words renders *one who serves behind the throne* or *occupies the throne aside to the throne of*

---

[21] Andrei A. Orlov, *From Patriarch to the Youth: The Metatron Tradition in 2 Enoch*, PhD diss. (Milwaukee: Marquette University, 2004), 124.

[22] This may be related to the Bavli's depiction of Metatron as the teacher of souls who died in their childhood. Avodah Zarah 3b states: "What then does God do in the fourth quarter? — He sits and instructs the school children, as it is said, Whom shall one teach knowledge, and whom shall one make to understand the message? Them that are weaned from the milk. Who instructed them theretofore? — If you like, you may say Metatron, or it may be said that God did this as well as other things. And what does He do by night? — If you like you may say, the kind of thing He does by day; or it may be said that He rides a light cherub, and floats in eighteen thousand worlds; for it is said, The chariots of God are myriads, even thousands shinan." See also 3 Enoch 48C:12 (Synopse 75) for a similar tradition.

[23] Hugo Odeberg, ed., *3 Enoch or The Hebrew Book of Enoch* (London: Cambridge University Press, 1929), 1.125, 1.126.

glory.[24] Gershom Scholem rejected this common view since the two terms did not appear separately in any text known he had encountered.[25]

The word σύνθρονος (synthronos) connotes a co-occupier of the divine throne. It is not, however, found in any source resources and consequently was rejected by Hugo Odeberg.[26] This is nevertheless supported by scholars Saul Lieberman and Peter Schäfer.[27] The Latin word Metator means messenger, guide, leader, or measurer.[28]

Philip Alexander notes Metatron's possible origin in the word, Metator, which occurs in Greek as *mitator*. This word refers to an officer in the Roman army who

---

[24] Andrei A. Orlov, *From Patriarch to the Youth: The Metatron Tradition in 2 Enoch,* PhD diss. (Milwaukee: Marquette University, 2004), 124. Gershom Scholem, *Major Trends in Jewish Mysticism* (New York: Schocken, 1995), 69.

[25] Gershom G. Scholem, *Jewish Gnosticism, Merkabah Mysticism, and Talmudic Tradition* (New York: Jewish Theological Seminary of America, 1960), 126. See Andrei A. Orlov, *From Patriarch to the Youth: The Metatron Tradition in 2 Enoch,* PhD diss. (Milwaukee: Marquette University, 2004), 124.

[26] Hugo Odeberg, *3 Enoch* (New York : Ktav Pub. House, 1973), 1.137.

[27] Peter Schäfer notes that " most probable is the etymology of Lieberman : Metatron = Greek metatronos = metathronos = synthronos: i.e. the small 'minor god,' whose throne is beside that of the great 'main God.'" Peter Schäfer, *The Hidden and Manifest God: Some Major Themes in Early Jewish Mysticism* (Albany: State University of New York Press, 1992), 29.

[28] This approach was suggested by Eleazar ben Judah of Worms, Rabbi Moshe ben Nachman, and discovered by Hugo Odeberg.

performed as a precursor or forerunner who goes ahead of a military column. Philip Alexander suggests the name may be related to the

> "the angel of the Lord who led the Israelites through the wilderness: acting like a Roman army *metator* guiding the Israelites on their way."[29]

The word μέτρον (metron, "a measure") has also been suggested as a possibility. Gedaliahu Stroumsa points to the fact that Metatron not only carries God's name, but he is also viewed as God's *Shi'ur Qomah* or the measurement of the divine body.[30]

Charles Mopsik suggests that Metatron's name may be related to Genesis 5:24, which states, "Enoch walked with God, then he was no more because God took him."[31] The Greek form of the Hebrew word "to take" is μετετέθη, i.e., meaning transferred.[32] רון (ron) is a standard addition to מטטרון (Metatron) and other angelic

---

[29] Philip Alexander, "From Son of Adam to a Second God: Transformation of the Biblical Enoch," in Biblical Figures Outside the Bible, ed. M. Stone and T. Bergen (Harrisburg, Penn.: Trinity Press, 1998), 107.

[30] Gedaliahu G. Stroumsa, "Form(s) of god: Some Notes on Metatron and Christ," Harvard Theological Review Volume 76, Issue 3 July (1983): 287.

[31] See C. Mopsik, *Le Livre hébreu d'Hénoch ou Livre des palais.* (Paris: Verdier, 1989).

[32] C. Mospik, *Le Livre hebreu d'Henoch ou Livre de palais* (Paris:Verdier, 1989), 48. Andrei A. Orlov, *From Patriarch to the Youth: The Metatron Tradition in 2 Enoch,* PhD diss. (Milwaukee: Marquette University, 2004), 128.

designations. According to Mopsik, מטט (MTT) is a transliteration from the Greek μετετέθη.

Joseph Dan suggests that the name Metatron may be connected to the latter's function. Metatron bears the name of God. Metatron is called the "lesser YHWH," which may be understood as a lesser manifestation of God's name. Joseph Dan interprets Exodus 23:21, which speaks of an exalted angel, who has God's name within him as being Metatron. God's name is what gives Metatron his rank and power. Dan notes that,

> "it appears that the reference here is to the letters tetra, i.e., the number four in Greek, a four-letter word in the middle of the name Metatron."[33]

Enoch as Metatron

All this was noted to help lay the foundation for the full Enoch story. The similarities between Enoch and Enmenduranki are significant. Enoch's lifespan of 365 years matches the number of days in a solar year, which coincides with the great concern of the *Astronomical Book* to ensure the proper calculation of the Biblical calendar (i.e., the solar calendar with the addition of appropriate days). I Enoch 82:4-5 states:

> "4 Blessed are all the righteous, blessed are all those who walk in the way of righteousness and sin not as the sinners, *in the reckoning of all their days in which the sun traverses the heaven,*

---

[33] Joseph Dan, *The Ancient Jewish Mysticism* (Jerusalem: Gefen Books: 1990), 109-110.

entering into and departing from the portals for thirty days with the heads of thousands of the order of the stars, together with the four which are intercalated which divide the four portions of the year, which 5 lead them and enter with them four days."

The calendar was a particular issue of concern for other groups. The *Book of Jubilees* not only embraced the solar calendar but also opposed the lunar one.

"There will be people who carefully observe the moon with lunar observations because it is corrupt (with respect to) the seasons and is early from year to year by ten days. Therefore years will come about for them when they will disturb (the year) and make a day of testimony something worthless and a profane day a festival. Everyone will join together both holy days with the profane and the profane day with the holy day, for they will err regarding the months, the Sabbaths, the festivals, and the jubilee."[34]

Enmenduranki also served as the priest of the sun-god. Both individuals are listed seventh in their respective genealogical lists. Both individuals are also credited with a special relationship to the divine. Both receive

---

[34] Book of Jubilees 6:36-37. James C. VanderKam, *Enoch: A Man for All Generations* (Columbia: University of South Carolina, 1995), 111.

unique knowledge as a consequence of their relationships.[35]

The place compared to his ancestors is also striking. If the numbers in Genesis 5:3-18 are summed, we can calculate that Enoch was born in the year 632. All of his ancestors were still alive at this stage, including Adam. Enoch is described as walking with God; none of his ancestors shares that designation.[36]

---

[35] James C. VanderKam, *Enoch: A Man for All Generations*, (Columbia: University of South Carolina, 1995), 9.

[36] Ibid., 11. The Greek version of the Wisdom of Sirach or Ecclesiasticus reads, "No one has been fashioned on the earth such as Enoch for he was also taken up from the earth." 44:14. Ibid., 107.

CHAPTER 4

Enoch the Seer

Divination or the practice of understanding the future through supernatural means through some ritual was very important in the Mesopotamian culture. The art of divination was a serious affair. In Mesopotamia, divination was practiced by highly-trained specialists. One of these groups was known as the *baru* guild. The guild was composed of oracle priests. The *baru* were seers as the name itself implies. The priests *saw* the future by interpreting the pattern of oil in water[1], by reviewing the arrangements of rising smoke, by examining the internal organs from sacrificed animals[2], and also from prophetic dreams.[3]

---

[1] The observation of the mixture of oil and water is referred to as lecanomancy.

[2] The inspection of the liver of a sacrificed animal is referred to as hepatoscopy.

[3] Andrei A. Orlov, *From Patriarch to the Youth: The Metatron Tradition in 2 Enoch,* PhD diss. (Milwaukee: Marquette University, 2004), 36.

Enmeduranki was imparted a divine secret from Anu, Enlil, and Ea via the gods Shamash, often referred to as the "lord of decisions," and Adad referred to as "lord of the oracle/omen."[4] Enmeduranki then transmitted these secrets to his son.[5] Future diviners, which are said to be descendants of Enmeduranki, also practiced this rite. The Nineveh text relates this,

> "When a diviner, and expert in oil, of abiding descent, offspring of Enmeduranki, king of Sippar, who set up the pure bowl and held the cedar-[-rod], a benediction priest of the king, a long-haired priest of Shamash as fashioned by Ninhursagga, begotten by a nissaku-priest of pure descent if he is without blemish in body and limbs he may have approached the presence of Shamash

---

[4] Anu was the supreme god and Enlil and Ea (Enki) were his sons. Andrei A. Orlov, *From Patriarch to the Youth: The Metatron Tradition in 2 Enoch,* PhD diss. (Milwaukee: Marquette University, 2004), 39.

[5] I Enoch 76:12 relates that "... and all their laws and all their plagues and all their benefactions have I shown to thee, my son Methuselah." Enoch 82:1 states: "1 And now, my son Methuselah, all these things I am recounting to thee and writing down for thee! and I have revealed to thee everything, and given thee books concerning all these: so preserve, my son Methuselah, the books from thy father's hand, and (see) that thou deliver them to the generations of the world." See also 81:5; 83:1, 10; 85:1; 91:1-2; 108:1. James Vanderkam states, "There is no mistaking the fact that Enoch relayed Uriel's revelations to Methuselah both orally and in writings." James Vanderkam, *Enoch and the Growth of an Apocalyptic Tradition* (Washington, D.C.: Catholic Biblical Association of America, 1984), 104.

and Adad were liver inspection and oracle (take place)."⁶

The term *beloved* highlights Enmeduranki's special relationship with the various gods. This special relationship is underscored because Enmeduranki was brought to the divine assembly's inner environs.⁷ The connection between Enmeduranki and Shamash and Adad is noteworthy for other reasons. Shamash was, as noted previously, the solar deity. Adad was the god of ====[=the weather. This element is important since Enoch is *introduced to astronomical and meteorological knowledge by the angel Uriel*. The *Astronomical Book* (I Enoch 72-82) relates the following:

> "The Book of the Motion of the Luminaries of the Heaven, how each one of them stands in relation to their number, to their powers and their times, of their names and their origins and their months, as the holy angel Uriel, who is their leader, *showed to me* when he was with me. *And he showed to* me their whole description as they are and for the

---

⁶ Translation by W. Lambert, "*Enmenduranki and Related Matters*", JCS 21 (1967): 132. Andrei A. Orlov, *From Patriarch to the Youth: The Metatron Tradition in 2 Enoch,* PhD diss. (Milwaukee: Marquette University, 2004), 37.

⁷ Andrei A. Orlov notes that later rabbinic literature including the *Peshikta de Rav* Kahana, written in the early medieval period, describes Enoch as beloved. The Midrash Ha-Gadol in turn, describes him as the beloved seventh. Andrei A. Orlov, *From Patriarch to the Youth: The Metatron Tradition in 2 Enoch,* PhD diss. (Milwaukee: Marquette University, 2004), 39.

years of the World to eternity, until the creation will be made anew to last forever."[8]

The text of Nineveh states that Shammash and Adad set Enmeduranki on a large throne of gold. Enmeduranki is elevated, and this elevation likely includes an exalted rank.[9] The Nineveh text describes Enmeduranki as the "the learned savant, who guards the secrets of the great gods."

In turn, Enoch is described as *yodea razim,* the Knower of Secrets in later Enoch-Metatron tradition.[10] The role of Enoch as a *Knower of Secret*s is intriguing. The fallen angel Azazel is condemned for having revealed eternal secrets. We will review the story of the

---

[8] 72:1; M. Black, *The Book of Enoch or I Enoch: A New English Edition*, SVTP 7 (Ledine: Brill, 1985).

[9] Andrei A. Orlov, *From Patriarch to the Youth: The Metatron Tradition in 2 Enoch,* PhD diss. (Milwaukee: Marquette University, 2004), 40. John J. Collins comment that "most significantly, Enoch is implicitly cast as a revealer of mysteries. The watchers are angels who descend to reveal a worthless mystery. Enoch is a human being who ascends to get true revelation." John J. Collins, "The Sage in Israel and the Ancient Near East" in John J. Collins, Seers, Sibyls, and Sages in Hellenistic-Roman Judaism (Leiden: Brill, 2001), 49.

[10] Andrei A. Orlov, *From Patriarch to the Youth: The Metatron Tradition in 2 Enoch,* PhD diss. (Milwaukee: Marquette University, 2004), 42. 3 EnochC:7 (Synopse 73) states "and I called him by name, the Lesser YHWH, Prince of the Divine Presence, and knower of secrets. Every secret I have revealed to him in love, every mystery I have made know to him in uprightness." Ibid., 138.

*Fallen Watcher*s in chapter twelve. For now, let us review I Enoch 9:6-7, which relates,

> "Thou seest what Azazel hath done, who hath taught all unrighteousness on earth and revealed the eternal secrets which were (preserved) in heaven, which men were striving to learn:"[11]

Christopher Rowland notes that this is peculiar since Enoch's reputation is partly based on his disclosure of heavenly secrets like astronomy. Unlike the angels, who acted on their initiative, Enoch receives these secrets through divine revelation. As Christopher Rowland concludes:

> "Enoch reveals exactly what he is told to reveal and, as a result, God only allows man to know sufficient for man's well-being. The angels, however, usurp God's right to reveal his mysteries and indulge in a profligate disclosure of the secrets of God."[12]

The shorter recension of 2 Enoch 40 relates one of the first episodes disclosing Enoch's unique insight. Enoch declares,

---

[11] In Greek mythology, Prometheus was a Titan. Prometheus created man and defied other gods by stealing fire and giving it to humans providing an interesting comparison to Azazel.

[12] Christopher Rowland, *The Open Heaven: A Study of Apocalyptic in Judaism and Early Christianity* (New York: Crossroad, 1982), 93-94.

"Now, therefore, my children, *I know everything*; some from the lips of the Lord, other my eyes have seen from the beginning to the end, and from the end to the recommencement."[13]

Andre Orlov summarizes Enoch and Metatron's critical differences, as found in I Enoch versus *Sefer Hekhalot*.

"...Metatron, unlike the earlier Enoch, not simply knows or writes down secrets, but embodies them, since some of the most profound mysteries are now literally written on him, or more specifically on his vestments, including his garments which recalls the Deity's own attire, the *Haluq*, and Metatron's glorious crown decorated by the secret letters inscribed by the hand of God."[14]

Sefer Hekhalot or 3 Enoch also relates the case of God's writing on Metatron's crown.

"Rabbi Ishmael said: Metatron, the angel, the Prince of the Presence, the Glory of all heavens, said to me:

(1) Because of the great love and mercy with which the Holy One, blessed be He, loved and

---

[13] Francis Andersen, "2 (Slavonic Apocalypse of) Enoch," in *The Old Testament Pseudepigrapha*, ed. J.H. Charlesworth (New York: Doubleday, 1985), 165.

[14] Andrei A. Orlov, *From Patriarch to the Youth: The Metatron Tradition in 2 Enoch,* PhD diss. (Milwaukee: Marquette University, 2004), 138.

cherished me more than all the children of heaven. He wrote with his finger with a flaming style upon the crown on my head the letters by which were created heaven and earth, the seas and rivers, the mountains and hills, the planets and constellations, the lightning, winds, earthquakes and voices (thunders), the snow and hail, the storm-wind and the tempest; the letters by which were created all the needs of the world and all the orders of Creation.

(2) And every single letter sent forth time after time as it were lightning, time after time as it were torches, time after time as it were flames of fire, time after time (rays) like [as] the rising of the sun and the moon and the planets."[15]

---

[15] 3 Enoch 13 (16). The significance of God's inscription on Metatron's crown is highlighted by Joseph Dan, "Metatron's crown, as that of God, is not only a source of light for the worlds, but represents the principal power of the one who carries it; creation. The highest stage pictured here states that God Himself engraved on Metatron's crown the letters with which the heaven and the earth and all their hosts were created. It thus follows that one who actually sees Metatron cannot but believe that he is standing before the one who carried out the actions with these letters, i.e., that the power inherent in them was utilized in the actual act of creation." Joseph Dan, *The Ancient Jewish Mysticism* (Jerusalem: Gefen Books: 1990), 139. The link between Metatron and creation has led some scholars to consider the possibility that Metatron may be a demiurge or at least a participant in creation. Nathaniel Deutsch, *Guardians of the Gate: Angelic Vice Regency in Late Antiquity* (Boston: Brill, 1998), 44-45.

Sefer Hekhalot 48D tells of the special secret Enoch-Metatron revealed to Moses.

> "YHWH, the God of Israel, is my witness that when *I revealed this secret to Moses*, all the armies of the height, in every heaven, were angry with me. They said to me, 'Why are you revealing this secret to humankind, born of woman, blemished, unclean, defiled by blood and impure flux, men who excrete putrid drops- that secret by which heaven and earth were created, the sea and the dry land, mountains and hills, rivers and springs, Gehinnom, fire and hail, the garden of Eden and the tree of life? By it Adam was formed, the cattle and the beasts of the field, the birds of heaven and the first of the sea, Behemoth and Leviathan, the unclean creatures and reptiles, the creepings things of the sea and the reptiles of the deserts, Torah, wisdom, knowledge, thought, the understanding of things above, and the fear of heave. Why are you revealing it to flesh and blood?"[16]

The *Astronomical Book* relates that cosmological, astronomical, and calendrical secrets were revealed to

---

[16] Philip Alexander, "3 (Hebrew Apocalypse of) Enoch," in *The Old Testament Pseudepigrapha*, ed., J.H. Charlesworth (New York: Doubleday, 1985), 315.

Enoch.[17] Nothing was withheld from Enoch as I Enoch 41:1-2 states:

> "And after that, I saw all the secrets of the heavens, and how the kingdom is divided, and how the actions of men are weighed in the balance."

There is an interesting similarity to this occurrence but related to Moses. *2 Baruch* is a Jewish pseudepigraphical work believed to have been written after the destruction of the Temple in Jerusalem in the first century CE. *2 Baruch* 59:5-12 states:

> "But he also showed him [Moses], at that time, the measures of fire, the depths of the abyss, the weight of the winds, the number of the raindrops, the suppression of wrath, the abundance of long-suffering, the truth of judgment, the root of wisdom, the richness of understanding, the fountain of knowledge, the height of the air, the greatness of Paradise, the ends of the periods, the beginning of the day of judgment, the number of offerings, the worlds which have not yet come, the mouth of hell, the standing place of vengeance, the place of faith, the region of hope,

---

[17] See I Enoch 72:1; 74:2; 80:1. Interestingly, Andrei Orlov notes that 2 Enoch is often titled with the term secret. i.e., *The Secret Books of Enoch, The Books called the secrets of God, a revelation of Enoch, The Book of the Secrets of Enoch, The Books of the Holy Secrets of Enoch,* etc. Andrei A. Orlov, *From Patriarch to the Youth: The Metatron Tradition in 2 Enoch,* PhD diss. (Milwaukee: Marquette University, 2004), 65.

the picture of the coming judgment, the multitude of angels which cannot be counted, the powers of the flame, the splendor of lightning, the voice of the thunders, the orders of the archangels, the treasures of the light, the changes of the times, and the inquiries into the Law."[18]

Enoch acquires this insight through various means, as indicated in the section of I Enoch titled the *Apocalypse of Weeks*[19] and in the Book of Watchers.[20] 3 Enoch or *Sefer Hekhalot* relates that God revealed all mysteries and secrets to Metatron, the transformed Enoch.

---

[18] A.F. J. Klijn, "2 (Syriac Apocalypse of) Baruch," in *The Old Testament Pseudepigrapha*, ed., J.H. Charlesworth (New York: Doubleday, 1985), 1.642.

[19] I Enoch 93:2 states: "According to that which appeared to me in the heavenly vision, And which I have known through the word of the holy angels, And have learnt from the heavenly tablets."

[20] I Enoch 71: 1-4 states: "1 And it came to pass after this *that my spirit was translated And it ascended into the heavens*: And I saw the holy sons of God. They were stepping on flames of fire: Their garments were white [and their raiment], And their faces shone like snow.2 And I saw two streams of fire, And the light of that fire shone like hyacinth, And I fell on my face before the Lord of Spirits.3 And the angel Michael [one of the archangels] seized me by my right hand, And lifted me up and led me forth into all the secrets, And he showed me all the secrets of righteousness. 4 And he showed me all the secrets of the ends of the heaven, And all the chambers of all the stars, and all the luminaries, Whence they proceed before the face of the holy ones." See also I Enoch 41:1-3; 46:2; 68:1.

"Rabbi Ishmael said: Metatron, the angel, the Prince of the Presence, said to me:

(1) Henceforth the Holy One, blessed be He, revealed to me all the mysteries of Tora and all the secrets of wisdom and all the depths of the Perfect Law; and all living beings' thoughts of the heart and all the secrets of the universe and all the secrets of Creation were revealed unto me even as they are revealed unto the Maker of Creation.

(2) And I watched intently to behold the secrets of the depth and the wonderful mystery. Before a man did think in secret, I saw (it), and before a man-made a thing, I beheld it."

(3) And there was no thing on high nor in the deep hidden from me."[21]

2 Enoch 50:1-7 extends the revelation of mysteries to Enoch to include man's hidden thoughts.

"1 I have put every man's work in writing and none born on earth can remain hidden, nor his works remain concealed.

2 I see all things.

3 Now, therefore, my children, in patience and meekness, spend the number of your days, that you inherit endless life.

---

[21] 3 Enoch 11:1-3. Translation of Hugo Odeberg.

4 Endure for the sake of the Lord every wound, every injury, every evil word and attack.

5 If ill-requitals befall you, return (them) not either to neighbor or enemy, because the Lord will return (them) for you and be your avenger on the day of great judgment, that there be no avenging here among men.

6 Whoever of you spends gold or silver for his brother's sake, he will receive ample treasure in the world to come.

7 Injure not widows nor orphans nor strangers, lest God's wrath come upon you."

The Nineveh text also reveals that Enmeduranki is given a tablet with the various secrets he is revealed. The tablet is then given to his son and the *baru* guild of diviners. The importance of the table is highlighted by Andrei Orlov when he states the following:

"The tablet is a medium that has the capacity to cross the boundaries between the upper and lower realms, as well as the boundaries of the generations. The two-fold function of the tablet as the instruments able to bridge the vertical (heavenly and celestial) and horizontal (antediluvian and postdiluvian) gaps makes it possible for it to remain a pivotal symbol of mediation prominent in the Mesopotamian and Enoch traditions."[22]

The Book of Enoch or I Enoch provides the first comparison to the Nineveh text. I Enoch 1:1-3 relates the following:

> "1 The words of the blessing of Enoch, wherewith he blessed the elect and righteous, who will be 2 living in the day of tribulation when all the wicked and godless are to be removed. And he took up his parable and said -Enoch a righteous man, whose eyes were opened by God, saw the vision of the Holy One in the heavens, which the angels showed me, and from them I heard everything, and from them I understood as I saw, but not for this generation, but for a remote one which is 3 for to come. Concerning the elect, I said, and took up my parable concerning them: The Holy Great One will come forth from His dwelling,"

For James Vanderkam, Enoch is described as a Jewish version of Enmeduranki. He is a mantic seer and diviner.[23] Vanderkam admits that despite the *likely influence* of Enmeduranki on the figure of Enoch, the figure found in Enochic literature is a diviner of a

---

[22] Andrei A. Orlov, *From Patriarch to the Youth: The Metatron Tradition in 2 Enoch* PhD diss. (Milwaukee: Marquette University, 2004), 44-45.

[23] James Vanderkam, *Enoch and the Growth of an Apocalyptic Tradition* (Washington, D.C.: Catholic Biblical Association of America, 1984), 116.

different sort who does not resort to lecanomancy or hepatoscopy.[24] Nevertheless, they share similarities in their interest in stars, dreams, and heavenly tablets. The *Baru* guild diviners were familiar with various divinatory techniques besides lecanomancy and hepatoscopy. The diviners were also familiar with extispicy, which analyzed entrails, ornithomancy, which analyzed birds' flight and different colorations in their skins, and libanomancy, which interpreted messages from rising smoke.[25] According to Alfred Haldar,

"the baru priests did not only interpret dreams; they also received revelation in them."[26]

---

[24] Perhaps most controversially James Vanderkam sees similarity between Enoch and Balaam the seer in Numbers 22-24. According to Vanderkam, Balaam is a diviner from the northern Euphrates area with ties to the Babylonian *Baru* guild of diviners. For Vanderkam, Enoch and Balaam, "Belong in mantic contexts, both speak under divine inspiration in such circumstances, and both pronounce future blessings upon the people of God and curses on their enemies." James Vanderkam, *Enoch and the Growth of an Apocalyptic Tradition* (Washington, D.C.: Catholic Biblical Association of America, 1984), 116, 118. See also Andrei A. Orlov, *From Patriarch to the Youth: The Metatron Tradition in 2 Enoch,* PhD diss. (Milwaukee: Marquette University, 2004), 53.

[25] John J. Collins, "The Sage in Israel and the Ancient Near East" in John J. Collins, Seers, Sibyls, and Sages in Hellenistic-Roman Judaism (Leiden: Brill, 2001), 347. Andrei A. Orlov, *From Patriarch to the Youth: The Metatron Tradition in 2 Enoch,* PhD diss. (Milwaukee: Marquette University, 2004), 54.

[26] Alfred Ossian Haldar, *Associations of Cult Prophets Among the Ancient Semites* (Uppsala: Almqvist & Wiksells, 1945), 7.

While there are similarities, there are also important distinctions. John J. Collins notes the following:

> "Enoch *does not employ* the techniques of the baru-consulting entrails, observing oil on water, or manipulating the cedar rod. The only Babylonian medium of revelation that he endorses is the dream, which had some precedent in biblical tradition (c. Jacob and Joseph), although it had also been subject to criticism. Interestingly, dream interpretation was not especially characteristic of the baru guild."[27]

Enoch and other biblical figures like Joseph and Daniel reject the typical forms associated with Egypt or Mesopotamia's religions. John Collins adds that Enoch and Daniel,

> "…too outdoes the Chaldeans at their own task of interpreting dreams and mysterious writings, *but he does so by the power of the God of Israel*. Daniel, like Enoch, endorses the dream as a medium of revelation but does not resort to the divinatory techniques of the *baru*. In each of these cases, the Jewish prophet or wise man is in competition with his Babylonian counterparts and accepts some of their presuppositions but also

---

[27] John J. Collins, "The Sage in Israel and the Ancient Near East" in John J. Collins, Seers, Sibyls, and Sages in Hellenistic-Roman Judaism (Leiden: Brill, 2001), 45. Collins also notes that Daniel 1-6 has Mesopotamian settings. Daniel is trained as a Babylonian sage and is even presented as a member of the association. Ibid., 46.

maintains a distinctive identity. The competitive aspect is not so explicit in the case of Enoch but is implied by the comparison with Enmeduranki."[28]

I Enoch relates the oneiromantic or dream activities of Enoch. I Enoch relates what occurred after Enoch's interaction with the Watchers. Enoch appears to receive an oracle by sleeping by a sacred spring.[29]

"And *I went off and sat down at the waters of Dan*, in the land of Dan, to the south of the west of Hermon: I read their petition till I fell 8 asleep. *And behold a dream came to me, and visions fell down upon me, and I saw visions of chastisement, and a voice came bidding (me)* I to tell it to the sons of heaven, and reprimand them. 9 And when I awaked, I came unto them, and they were all sitting gathered together, weeping in 10 'Abelsjail, which is between Lebanon and Seneser, with their faces covered. And I recounted before them all the visions which I had seen in sleep, and I began to speak the words of

---

[28] John J. Collins, "The Sage in Israel and the Ancient Near East" in John J. Collins, Seers, Sibyls, and Sages in Hellenistic-Roman Judaism (Leiden: Brill, 2001), 46.

[29] J.S.Hanson, "Dreams and Visions in the Graeco-Roman World and Early Christianity," in Aufstieg and Niedergang der Romischen Welt II (Berlin: Walter de Gruyter, 1980), 1395-1427. I Enoch 83:3 and I Enoch 86:1 relates that the visions that Enoch experienced were received in dreams.

righteousness, and to reprimand the heavenly Watchers."[30]

The *Book of Jubilees* also relates a vision that Enoch received during sleep. The *Book of Jubilees* 4:19 relates:

> "And what was and what will be he saw in a vision of his sleep, as it will happen to the children of men throughout their generations until the Day of Judgment; he saw and understood everything, and wrote his testimony, and placed the testimony on earth for all the children of men and for their generations."

Like Joseph and Daniel, Enoch not only experienced visions but also interpreted dreams for others. The *Book of Giants* relates the story that dreams tormented the Giants, the illicit union's offspring between the Fallen Watchers and women. Various fragments of this book were found at Qumran.[31]

> "Thereupon two of them had dreams 4 and the sleep of their eye, fled from them, and they arose and came to [. . . and told] their dreams, and said in the assembly of [their comrades] the monsters 6[. . . In] my dream I was watching this very night 7[and

---

[30] I Enoch 3:7-9.

[31] 4Q203, 1Q23, 2Q26, 4Q530-532, 6Q8. In addition, five separate Aramaic manuscripts of the *Book of Watchers* were found at Qumran. Annette Yoshiko Reed, *Fallen Angels and the History of Judaism and Christianity* (Cambridge: Cambridge Press, 2004), 7.

> there was a garden . . .] gardeners and they were watering 8[. . . two hundred trees and] large shoots came out of their root 9[. . .] all the water, and the fire burned all 10[the garden . . .] They found the giants to tell them 11[the dream . . .]"[32]

Unsettled by the dreams, they try to find someone to interpret the dreams but are unsuccessful. The giants decide to go to Enoch, the scribe of distinction. The *Book of Watchers* continues with the following:

> [. . . to Enoch] the noted scribe, and he will interpret for us 12 the dream. Thereupon his fellow Ohya declared and said to the giants, 13 I too had a dream this night, O giants, and, behold, the Ruler of Heaven came down to earth 14[. . .] and such is the end of the dream. [Thereupon] all the giants [and monsters! grew afraid 15and called Mahway. He came to them, and the giants pleaded with him and sent him to Enoch 16[the noted scribe]. They said to him, Go [. . .] to you that 17[. . .] you have heard his voice. And he said to him, He will [. . . and] interpret the dreams [. . .] Col. 3 3[. . .] how long the Giants have to live. [. . .][33]

---

[32] http://www.gnosis.org/library/dss/dss_book_of_giants.htm

[33] "[...] The Giants could [not] find (someone) to explain to the[m] [the dream...to Enoch,] the scribe of distinction, and he will interpret the dream for us." 4 Q530ii. 13-14.

CHAPTER 5

Enoch the Scribe

Enmeduranki is not explicitly designated as a scribe in the Nineveh text. There are, however, indirect references that link the exalted hero with the office of a scribe. As was previously noted, Enmeduranki receives a tablet of the gods, which includes the secrets for divination.

I Enoch 74:2 describes Enoch's response to the angel Uriel revealing the sun and moon's motion.

> "And all these Uriel, the holy angel who is the leader of them all, showed to me, and their positions and *I wrote down their positions as he showed them to me*, and *I wrote down their months* 3 as they were, and the appearance of their lights till fifteen days were accomplished."

Enoch is explicitly referred to as a scribe in various sections of Enochic literature. The Qumran Scrolls include the text labeled 4Q203 8, which states the following:

"copy of the seco[n]d tablet of [the] le[tter...] by the hand of Enoch, *the distinguished scribe...*"[1]

I Enoch 81:1-6 refers to the heavenly tablets and the instructions given to Enoch by the angels that bring him back to earth. Enoch is to record/copy the tablets for this son Methuselah.

> "1 And he said unto me: ' Observe, Enoch, these heavenly tablets, and read what is written thereon, And mark every individual fact.'
>
> 2 And I observed the heavenly tablets, and read everything which was written (thereon) and understood everything, and read the book of all the deeds of mankind, and of all the children of flesh 3 that shall be upon the earth to the remotest generations. And forthwith I blessed the great Lord the King of glory forever, in that He has made all the works of the world,
>
> And I extolled the Lord because of His patience And blessed Him because of the children of men.
>
> 4 And after that, I said: ' Blessed is the man who dies in righteousness and goodness, Concerning whom there is no book of unrighteousness written, And against whom no day of judgment shall be found.'

---

[1] F. Garcia Martinez and Eibert J.C. Tigchelaar (eds.), *The Dead Sea Scrolls Study Edition Volume 1* (Leiden: Brill, 1997), 411.

5 And those seven holy ones brought me and placed me on the earth before the door of my house, and said to me: ' Declare everything to thy son Methuselah, and show to all thy children that no 6 flesh is righteous in the sight of the Lord, for He is their Creator. One year we will leave thee with thy son, till thou givest thy (last) commands, that thou mayest teach thy children *and record (it) for them,* and testify to all thy children; and in the second year they shall take thee from their midst."

Enoch records the contents from the heavenly tablets to transfer this knowledge to his son. Similarly, Enmeduranki instructs his son concerning the divine secrets that have been disclosed to him. He also transfers to his son a tablet and a stylus, the tool of the scribe. The Nineveh text states:

"the learned savant, who guards the secrets of the great gods, will bring his son whom he loves with an oath before Shamash and Adad by tablet and stylus and will instruct him."[2]

The identification of Enoch as a scribe was likely tied to his designation as a sage. I Enoch relates the importance of wisdom when Enoch transmits his newly acquired knowledge to his son Methuselah.

---

[2] Translation by W. Lambert, *"Enmenduranki and Related Matters"*, JCS 21 (1967): 132. See also Andrei A. Orlov, *From Patriarch to the Youth: The Metatron Tradition in 2 Enoch,* PhD diss. (Milwaukee: Marquette University, 2004), 46.

"1 And now, my son Methuselah, all these things I am recounting to thee and writing down for thee! And I have revealed to thee everything, and given thee books concerning all these: so preserve, my son Methuselah, the books from thy father's hand, and (see) that thou deliver them to the generations of the world.

2 *I have given Wisdom to thee and to thy children*, [And thy children that shall be to thee], That they may give it to their children for generations, *This wisdom (namely) that passeth their thought.*

3 *And those who understand it shall not sleep, But shall listen with the ear that they may learn this wisdom*, And it shall please those that eat thereof better than good food."[3]

2 Enoch also continues this description of Enoch as a scribe. 2 Enoch 10 states:

"And the Lord summoned one of his archangels by name Pravuil[4], whose knowledge was quicker in

---

[3] I Enoch 82:2-3. The idea of Enoch as a man of wisdom is articulated by the scholar Martin Hengel when he stated, "Enoch appears as the prototype of the pious wise man of the primal period....A whole series of features of the Babylonian wise men of the primal period were transferred to his figure, which probably derives from the Babylonian primal king Enmeduranki." Martin Hengel, *Judaism and Hellenism: studies in their encounter in Palestine during the Early Hellenistic Period Volume 1* (Eugene: Wipf and Stock Publishers, 2003), 204.

[4] Pravuil is often rendered as Vereveil.

wisdom than the other archangels, who wrote all the deeds of the Lord; and the Lord said to Pravuil: Bring out the books from my store-houses, and a reed of quick-writing, and give it to Enoch, and deliver to him the choice and comforting books out of your hand."[5]

The description of Enoch as a scribe is reinforced in 2 Enoch 23:2-3.

"2 And Pravuil told me: All the things that I have told you, we have written. *Sit and write all the souls of mankind*, however many of them are born, and the places prepared for them to eternity; for all souls are prepared to eternity, before the formation of the world.

3 *And all double thirty days and thirty nights, and I wrote out all things exactly, and wrote three hundred and sixty-six books.*"[6]

---

[5] 2 Enoch 22:10.

[6] The *Testament of Abraham* is an apocalyptic pseudepigraphic work. It was probably written in the 1st or 2nd century CE. It describes Enoch as a scribe which records the actions of man for the purposes of judgment. Section 11 states, "11. And Abraham said to Michael, Lord, who is this judge, and who is the other, who convicts the sins? And Michael said to Abraham, Do you see the judge? This is Abel, who first testified, and God brought him hither to judge, and he that bears witness here is the teacher of heaven and earth, and the scribe of righteousness, Enoch, for the Lord sent them hither to write down the sins and righteousnesses of each one." https://goo.gl/FSGx2s

The wisdom that Enoch transmits to his son is worthy enough to be shared throughout the generations, as verse 2 makes clear. The Cairo Genizah Hebrew version of the Wisdom of Sirach confirms the importance of Enoch's understanding by stating that Enoch is *ot da'at l'dor v'dor* – a sign of knowledge from generation to generation.[7] Enoch's knowledge is supernal, but it is also practical and this-worldly. The *Book of Jubilees* relates Enoch's skills.

> "And he was the first among men that are born on earth who learnt writing and knowledge and wisdom and who wrote down the signs of heaven according to the order of their months in a book, that men might know the seasons of the years according to the order of their separate months."[8]

The *Book of Giants* found at Qumran describes Enoch as the *scribe of distinction* and *the distinguished scribe.*[9]

---

[7] Cairo Geniza MS Ben Sira 44:16. See also Andrei A. Orlov, *From Patriarch to the Youth: The Metatron Tradition in 2 Enoch,* PhD diss. (Milwaukee: Marquette University, 2004), 60.

[8] Book of Jubilees 4:17.

[9] Book of Giants 4Q203 8:4 and 4Q530ii.14. An older recension of the Ethiopic version of the Book of Enoch uses the terms "skilled scribe" or "scribe of all skill. Andrei Orlov points out that this may be related to the term *sofer mahir*, i.e., the ready scribe, used in the Hebrew Bible. Ezra 7:6 states, "...this Ezra went up from Babylon; and he was a ready scribe in the Law of Moses, which the LORD, the God of Israel, had given." Psalm 45:2 states, "My heart overfloweth with a goodly matter; I say: 'My work is concerning a king'; my tongue is the pen of a ready

The Babylonian Talmud also preserves the image of Metatron as a scribe. However, the identification with Enoch is not assumed in this passage.[10] Nor is Metatron's position as scribe assumed to be necessarily positive. The Bavli in Tractate Hagigah 15a states:

> "He saw the angel Metatron, who was granted permission to sit and write the merits of Israel. He said: There is a tradition that in the world above there is no sitting; no competition; no turning one's back before Him, i.e., all face the Divine Presence; and no lethargy. Seeing that someone other than God was seated above, he said: Perhaps, the Gemara here interjects, Heaven forbid, there are two authorities, and there is another source of power in control of the world in addition to God."[11]

---

writer." See also Andrei A. Orlov, *From Patriarch to the Youth: The Metatron Tradition in 2 Enoch,* PhD diss. (Milwaukee: Marquette University, 2004), 76.

[10] Regarding this, Philip Alexander states: "It is not clear when Metatron absorbed the Enoch tradition. In an attributed stratum of the Babli (b. Hag. 15a) it is stated that 'permission was granted to Metatron to site and write down the merits of Israel.' This scribing role of Metatron may have been taken over from the Enoch traditions which portray Enoch as the heavenly scribe (Jub 4:23; Ps-J Gen. 5:24)…" Philip Alexander, "The Historical Settings of the Hebrew Book of Enoch," JJS 28 (1977): 164.

[11] The William Davidson Talmud Hagiga 15a. https://goo.gl/xN6a9c

Sefer Hekhalot or 3 Enoch also relates the evolution of Enoch-Metatron's role as a heavenly scribe to an assistant to God in divine judgment.

> "At first I sat upon a great throne at the door of the seventh place, and I judged all the denizens of the heights on the authority of the Holy One, blessed be he...when I at in the heavenly court. The princes of kingdoms stood beside me, to my right and to my left by the authority of the Holy One, blessed be he...when I sat in the heavenly court. The prince of kingdoms stood beside me, to my right and to my left, by authority of the Holy One, blessed be he. But when Aher came to behold the vision of the chariot and set eyes upon me, he was afraid and trembled before me. His soul was alarmed to the pointing of leaving him, because of his fear, dread, and terror of me, when he saw me seated upon a throne like a king, with ministering angels standing beside me as servants and all the princes of kingdoms crowned with crowns surrounding me."[12]

Christopher Rowland relates the intertwined role of the scribe with that of the heavenly witness. Rowland states,

> "in Hebrew Enoch Metatron is a judge in the heavenly court, whereas in B [Babylonian

---

[12] 3 Enoch 16:1-5. Andrei Orlov comments that Enoch –Metatron has not transitioned to the position of celestial judicator. Andrei A. Orlov, *From Patriarch to the Youth: The Metatron Tradition in 2 Enoch,* PhD diss. (Milwaukee: Marquette University, 2004), 149.

Hagigah 15a] he is merely the heavenly scribe who records the merits of Israel. The different pictures of Metatron reflect the different versions of the Enoch-tradition. Enoch's position as a scribe and a heavenly witness belong to the oldest part of the tradition (Jubilees 4:23; the Testament of Abraham Recension B 11; I Enoch 12; Targum Pseudo-Jonathan on Gen. 5.24). On the other hand, we have evidence of Enoch as a supremely more exalted figure…In B. however, it seems that Metatron sits close to God recording the merits of Israel."[13]

The Targum Pseudo-Jonathan, an Aramaic translation of the Bible, on Genesis 5:24, provides a fantastic commentary of Enoch in equating him with none other than Metraton, the principal angel of rabbinic lore.

"Enoch worshipped in truth before the Lord after he had begotten Methuselah three hundred years, and he begot sons and daughters. All the days of Enoch with the inhabitants of the earth were three hundred and sixty-five years. Enoch worshipped in truth before the Lord, and behold, he was not with the inhabitants of the earth because he was taken away, and he ascended to the firmament at

---

[13] Christopher Roland, *The Open Heaven: A Study in Apocalypticism in Judaism and Early Christianity* (Eugene: Wipf and Stock Publishers, 2002), 336-337.

the command of the Lord. And he was called Metraton, the Great Scribe."[14]

---

[14] M. Maher, *Targum Pseudo-Jonathan: Genesis. Aramaic Bible 1B*. (Collegeville: Liturgical Press, 1992).

CHAPTER 6

Enoch the Priest

The office of priest is not explicitly assigned to Enmeduranki. The assumption of priestly duties is not a significant stretch, however. The *baru* guild of diviners was closely associated with sacerdotal duties. That the priesthood was related to Enmeduranki at least by tradition is confirmed in another text related to Nebuchadnezzar I. The text dated between 1125BCE and 1104 BCE reads as follows:

> "...king of Babylon who *supervises all the cult-centers and confirms the regular offerings*, am I, distant scion of kingship, seed preserved from before the flood, offspring of [Enmeduranki], king of Sippar, who set up the pure bowl and held the cedar-wood (rod), who sat in the presence of Shamash and Adad, the divine adjudicators, foremost son, [...] king of justice, reliable

shepherd, who keeps the land's foundations secure."[1]

The *baru* guild was a priestly group that emphasized ritual purity on an ongoing basis. Similar to the requirements stipulated in the book of Leviticus, the Mesopotamian priests had to be free of certain physical defects.[2] They could not have defective eyes or maimed fingers.[3] The Nineveh tablet relates that Shamash appointed Enmeduranki.

> "Samas in *Ebabbara* [appointed] Enmeduranki [king of Sippar]"[4]

According to Andrei Orlov, Ebabbarra refers to the house of the rising sun. This connotes the temple of Shamash. The Nineveh text continues by references the offspring of Enmeduranki as a priest who may approach Shamash and Adad's presence.[5] Andrei Orlov notes the importance of this statement on Enmeduranki's priestly connection.

> "The idea that Enmeduranki's initiation into the assembly of the gods might mark the beginning

---

[1] Translation by W. Lambert, "*Enmenduranki and Related Matters*", JCS 21 (1967): 130.

[2] See Leviticus 21:17-23.

[3] Andrei A. Orlov, *From Patriarch to the Youth: The Metatron Tradition in 2 Enoch,* PhD diss. (Milwaukee: Marquette University, 2004), 47-48.

[4] Translation by W. Lambert, "*Enmenduranki and Related Matters*", JCS 21 (1967): 126-138.

[5] Nineveh text line 22-29.

of the priestly line is significant for a possible association of the king with the priestly office."[6]

In contrast to the future priests who may enter Shamash and Adad's presence if they are ritually acceptable, Endmeduranki is already seated in their company.[7]

Enoch is presented as a priest in Enochic literature. Still, the emphasis is placed on his role in a celestial temple. According to Martha Himmelfarb, Enoch's journey in the celestial sphere reflects his visit to a heavenly temple.[8] I Enoch 14:9-19 states the following:

---

[6] Andrei A. Orlov, *From Patriarch to the Youth: The Metatron Tradition in 2 Enoch,* PhD diss. (Milwaukee: Marquette University, 2004), 49.

[7] Ibid., 50.

[8] M. Himmelfarb, "The Temple and the Garden of Eden in Ezekiel, the Book of Watchers, and the Wisdom of ben Sira," in *Sacred Places and Profane Spaces: Essays in the Geographics of Judaism, Christianity, and Islam*, eds. J. Scott and P. Simpson-Housely (New York: Greenwood Press, 1991), 63-78. Martha Himmelfarb notes that "more clearly in the Greek, but also in the Ethiopic this arrangement echoes the structure of the earthly temple with its vestibule (*ulam*), sanctuary (*hekhal*), and holy of holies (*dvir*)." Martha Himmelfarb, "Apocalyptic Ascent and the Heavenly Temple," in Society of Biblical Literature 1987 Seminars Papers SBLSP 26 (Atlanta: Scholars Press, 1987), 210. The interpretation of I Enoch 14 as tour of the heavenly temple by Enoch is supported by George Nickelsburg, who sees the large house as a temple. He also references 12:4 and 15:3 which refer to an eternal sanctuary. Finally, Nickelsburg contends that the language about the fallen angels as well as the angels which approach God indicates that some angels function as priests. George W.E. Nickelsburg, "Enoch, Levi, and Peter : recipients of

"And I went in till I drew nigh to a wall which is built of crystals and surrounded by tongues of fire: and it began to affright 10 me. And I went into the tongues of fire and drew nigh to a large house which was built of crystals: and the walls of the house were like a tesselated floor (made) of crystals, and its groundwork was 11 of crystal. Its ceiling was like the path of the stars and the lightnings, and between them were 12 fiery cherubim, and their heaven was (clear as) water. A flaming fire surrounded the walls, and its 13 portals blazed with fire. And I entered into that house, and it was hot as fire and cold as ice: there 14 were no delights of life therein: fear covered me, and trembling got hold upon me. And as I quaked 15 and trembled, I fell upon my face. And I beheld a vision, And lo! there was a second house, greater 16 than the former, and the entire portal stood open before me, and it was built of flames of fire. And in every respect, it so excelled in splendor and magnificence and extent that I cannot describe to 17 you its splendor and its extent. And its floor was of fire, and above it were lightnings and the path 18 of the stars, and its ceiling also was flaming fire. And I looked and saw therein a lofty throne: its appearance was as

---

revelation in upper Galilee," Journal of Biblical Literature 100,4 (1981): 580-581.

crystal, and the wheels thereof as the shining sun, and there was the vision of 19 cherubim."

Andrei Orlov notes that God's throne is situated in the inmost chamber of this construction. The cherubim denote the throne in 14:18.[9] Accordingly, it may be regarded as a heavenly complement to the cherubim found in the Holy of Holies in the Temple in Jerusalem. The *Animal Apocalypse* 89: 50 states:

> "50 And that house became great and broad, and it was built for those sheep: (and) a tower lofty and great was built on the house for the Lord of the sheep, and that house was low, but the tower was elevated and lofty, and the Lord of the sheep stood on that tower, and they offered a full table before Him."

According to Michael Knibb, the term *house* is reserved within the Animal Apocalypse for a temple.[10] While the *Book of Enoch* only alludes to Enoch's priestly role, the *Book of Jubilees* explicitly mentions this.

> "And on account of it (God) brought the waters of the flood upon all the land of Eden; for there he was set as a sign and that he should testify against all the children of men, that he should recount all

---

[9] Regarding the Cherubim, see Exodus 26:1, 31; 36:8, 35. See also I Kings 6:29, 2 Chronicles 3:7; Ezekiel 41:15-26.

[10] James C. VanderKam, *Enoch: A Man for All Generations* (Columbia: University of South Carolina, 1995), 117.

the deeds of the generations until the day of condemnation.

And he burnt the incense of the sanctuary, (even) sweet spices acceptable before the Lord on the Mount."[11]

Metatron is explicitly called a priest in a fragment from the Cairo Genizah. The fragment reads:

"I adjure you [Metatron], more beloved and dear than all heavenly beings, [Faithful servant] of the God of Israel, the High Priest, chief of [the priest]s, you who poss[ess seven]ty names; and whose name [is like your Master's]...Great Prince, who is appointed over the great princes, who is the head of all the camps."[12]

The tradition of Enoch-Metatron serving in a priestly role is further confirmed in *Sefer Hekhalot*. 3 Enoch 15B relates the following:

---

[11] *Book of Jubilees* 4: 24-25.

[12] L. H. Schiffmann and M. D. Swartz, *Hebrew and Aramaic Incantation Texts from the Cairo Genizah* (Sheffield: Sheffield Academic Press, 1992), 145. Sefer Hekhalot or 3 Enoch states: "(1) R. Ishmael said: Said to me Metatron, the Prince of the Presence and the prince over all the princes and he stands before Him who is greater than all the Elohim. And he goes in under the Throne of Glory. And he has a great tabernacle of light on high. And he brings forth the fire of deafness and puts (it) into the ears of the Holy Chayyoth, that they may not hear the voice of the Word (Dibbur) that goes forth from the mouth of the Divine Majesty. Translation of Hugo Odeberg.

"Metatron is the Prince over all the princes and stands before him who is exalted above all gods. He goes beneath the throne of glory, where he has a great heavenly tabernacle of light, and brings out the deafening fire, and puts it in the ears of the holy creature so that they should not hear the sound of the utterance that issues from the mouth of the Almighty."[13]

Enoch-Metatron is granted access to the realm of God's presence much in the same way that the earthly *Cohen Gadol*, i.e., the high priest, stepped behind the curtain to enter the holy of holies. Enoch-Metatron also serves as another function. He serves as the coordinator of the heavenly hosts who acclaim God through liturgical praise. Metatron protects the celestial singers by protecting their ears since God's voice is so powerful that it will injure them. Andrei Orlov observes:

---

[13] Philip Alexander, "3 (Hebrew Apocalypse of) Enoch," in *The Old Testament Pseudepigrapha*, ed., J.H. Charlesworth (New York: Doubleday, 1985), 303. See Andrei A. Orlov, *From Patriarch to the Youth: The Metatron Tradition in 2 Enoch*, PhD diss. (Milwaukee: Marquette University, 2004), 153. The tradition of Metatron serving as a priest in the heavenly tabernacle is also found in the Mandean inscription on a bowl which describes Metatron as the one "who serves before the Curtain." W.S. McCullough, *Jewish and Mandean Incantation Texts in the Royal Ontario Museum* (Toronto: University of Toronto Press, 1967), D 5-6.

> "The depiction of the angelic hosts as unable to sustain the terrifying sound of God's voice or the terrifying vision of God's glorious Face is not a rare motif in the Hekhalot writings. In such the descriptions Metatron usually poses as the mediator par excellence who protests the angelic hosts participating in the heavenly liturgy against the dangers of the direct encounter with the divine presence. This combination of the liturgical duties with the role of Prince of Presence appears to be a long-lasting tradition with its possible roots in the Second Temple Judaism."[14]

Metatron's depiction as a heavenly priest is not limited to Jewish mystical literature. The midrash known as *Numbers Rabbah* contains a passage which also links Metatron with the tabernacle.

> "Rabbi Simon expounded: When the Holy One, blessed be He, told Israel to set up the Tabernacle. He intimated to the ministering angels that they also should make a Tabernacle, and when the one below was erected, the other was erected on high. The latter was the tabernacle of the youth whose name was Metatron, and therein he offers up the souls of the righteous to atone for Israel in the days of their exile."[15]

---

[14] Andrei A. Orlov, *From Patriarch to the Youth: The Metatron Tradition in 2 Enoch,* PhD diss. (Milwaukee: Marquette University, 2004), 50.

[15] Numbers Rabbah 12:12; Midrash Rabbah, 5.482-3.

This image of Enoch is also found in the Zohar[16] and a text found in the famous Cairo Genizah.[17] The idea of Metatron as a heavenly high priest may rest in part on the widespread view that Michael, the archangel, also served as a heavenly priest. The Bavli, in Hagigah 12b, states that Michael, "the great minister, stands and sacrifices an offering upon it, as it is stated: "I have surely built a house of Zevul for You, a place for You to dwell forever" (I Kings 8:13)." Tractate Menahot 110 also relates, that "Rav Giddel says that Rav says: This is referring to the altar that remains built-in Heaven even after the earthly Temple was destroyed, and the angel Michael, the great minister, stands and sacrifices an offering upon it." Finally, Tractate Zevachim 62a states: "They saw a vision of the altar already built and Michael the archangel standing and sacrificing offerings upon

---

[16] Zohar II, 159a states, "We have learned that the Holy One, blessed be He, told Moses all the regulations and the patterns of the Tabernacle, each one with its own prescription, and [Moses] saw Metatron ministering as High Priest with within...he saw Metatron ministering...The Holy One, blessed be He, said to Moses: Look at the tabernacle, and the look at the boy..." Isaiah Tishby, *The Wisdom of the Zohar: An Anthology of Texts: Volume 2* (Liverpool: Littman Library Of Jewish Civilization, 1989), 645.

[17] "I adjure you [Metatron], more beloved and dear than all heavenly beings, [Faithful servant] of God of Israel, the High Priest, chief of [the priests, you who poss[ess seven]ty names; and whose name [is like your Master's] ...Great Prince, who is appointed over the great princes, who is the head of all the camps." L. H. Schiffman and M.D. Swartz, *Hebrew and Aramaic Incantation Texts from the Cairo Genizah* (Shefflield: Sheffield Academix Press, 1992), 145-7, 151.

it."[18] Enoch-Metatron serves as the vehicle through which praises to God flow.

> "When the youth enters below the throne of glory, God embraces him with a shining face. All the angels gather and address God as 'the great, mighty, awesome God,' and they praise God three times a day by means of the youth."[19]

---

[18] Martin Cohen argued that based on the *Shi'ur Qomah* that Metatron function was more of a heavenly choir director and beadle than that of a high priest. Martin S. Cohen, *Shiur Qomah: Liturgy and Theurgy in Pre-Kabbalistic Jewish Mysticism* (New York: University Press Of America, 1983), 134. The Hekhalot Zutarti (Synopse 390) also points to Metatron's liturgical role. "One hayyah rises above the seraphim and descends upon the tabernacle of the youth whose name is Metatron, and speaks with a loud voice. A voice of sheer silence…Suddenly the angels fall silent. The watchers and holy ones become quiet. They are silent, and are pushed into the river of fire. The hayyot put their faces on the ground, and this youth whose name is Metatron brings the fire of deafness and puts it into their ears so that they could not hear the sound of God's speech or the ineffable name. The youth whose name is Metatron then invokes, in seven voices, his living, pure, honored, awesome…name." Peter Schafer, ed., *Synopse Zur Hekhalot-Literatur* (Tübingen: Mohr Siebeck, 1991), 164.

[19] Peter Schafer, ed., *Synopse Zur Hekhalot-Literatur* (Tübingen: Mohr Siebeck, 1991), 162-163. Metatron's liturgical role is alluded to in the longer recension of 2 Enoch 18:8 which states, "And I [Enoch] said, 'Why are you waiting for your brothers? And why don't you perform the liturgy before the face of the Lord? Start up your liturgy, and perform the liturgy before the face of the Lord, so that you do not enrage your Lord to the limit." F.I. Andersen, '2 (Slavonic Apocalypse of) Enoch', in J.H. Charlesworth, ed., *The Old Testament Pseudepigrapha Volume*

The ascription of the title Youth to Enoch is partly based on the Proverbs 22:6, which states:

חֲנֹךְ לַנַּעַר, עַל-פִּי דַרְכּוֹ-- גַּם כִּי-יַזְקִין, לֹא-יָסוּר מִמֶּנָּה.

The first two words read, *Hanoch laNa'ar*, i.e., Enoch turned into the Youth, or Metatron. 2 Enoch 24 relates an encounter between God and Enoch.

"1 And the Lord summoned me and said to me: Enoch, sit down on my left with Gabriel.

2 And I bowed down to the Lord, and the Lord spoke to me: Enoch, beloved, all (that) you see, all things that are standing finished I tell to you even before the very beginning, all that I created from non-being, and visible (physical) things from invisible (spiritual).

3 Hear, Enoch, and take in these my words, for not to My angels have I told my secret, and I have not told them their rise, nor my endless realm, nor have they understood my creating, which I tell you today."

1: Apocalyptic Literature and Testaments (New York: Doubleday, 1985), 132.

CHAPTER 7

Enoch and the Prince of the Presence

The *Sefer Hekhalot* introduces us to a unique title in the litany of previous designations given to Enoch-Metatron. In *Sefer Hekhalot,* he is referred to as the *Sar haPanim*, the Prince of the Presence, or the Faces. Enoch-Metatron is the angelic figure who has access to the Divine Presence, or the Face of the Godhead.[1]

---

[1] Andrei A. Orlov, *From Patriarch to the Youth: The Metatron Tradition in 2 Enoch,* PhD diss. (Milwaukee: Marquette University, 2004), 163. 3 Enoch 8:1 states, "Rabbi Ishmael said: Metatron, the Prince of the Presence, said to me: (1) Before He appointed me to attend the Throne of Glory, the Holy One, blessed be He, opened to me three hundred thousand gates of Understanding, three hundred thousand gates of Subtlety, three hundred thousand gates of Life, three hundred thousand gates of grace and loving-kindness, three hundred thousand gates of love, three hundred thousand gates of Tora, three hundred thousand gates of meekness, three hundred thousand gates of maintenance,

This tradition may be related to the view that God created Adam in His likeness. 2 Enoch 44:1 states:

> "1 The Lord with his hands having created man, *in the likeness of his own face*, the Lord made him small and great."[2]

In *Sefer Hekhalot,* Enoch-Metatron's unparalleled access to God's presence is demonstrated when he protects Rabbi Ishmael from the other angels and brings him into the Divine presence.

> "At once the Holy One, blessed be he, summoned to my aid his servant, the angel Metatron, Prince of the Divine Presence. He flew out to meet me

---

three hundred thousand gates' of mercy, three hundred thousand gates of fear of heaven." See Isaiah 63:9.

[2] Genesis Rabbah 11 sheds light on Adam's garments. "Adam's glory did not abide the night with him. What is the proof? But Adam passeth not the night in glory (Ps. XLIX, 13). The Rabbis maintain, 'His glory abode with him, but at the termination of the Sabbath He deprived him of his splendor and expelled him from the Garden of Eden, as it is written, Thou changest his countenance, and sendest him away (Job XIV, 20)." Leviticus Rabbah 20:2 also states the following: "Resh Lakish, in the name of R. Simeon the son of Menasya, said: 'The apple of Adam's heel outshone the globe of the sun; how much more so the brightness of this face! Nor need you wonder. In the ordinary way if a person makes salvers, one for himself and one for his household, whose will he make more beautiful? Not his own? Similarly, Adam was created for the service of the Holy One, blessed be He, and the globe of the sun for the service of mankind." H. Freedman and M. Simon, Midrash Rabbah, 4.252.

with great alacrity, to save me from their power. He grasped me with his hand before their eyes and said to me, 'Come in peace into the presence of the high and exalted King to behold the likeness of the chariot.'"[3]

The unique position that Enoch-Metatron holds as *Prince of the Presence* is highlighted by the transformation Enoch went through in becoming Metatron. *Sefer Hekhalot* describes this process.

"Rabbi Ishmael said: The angel Metatron, Prince of the Divine Presence, the glory of highest heaven, said to me: When the Holy One, blessed be He, took me to serve the throne of glory, the wheels of the chariot and all the needs of the Shekinah, at once my flesh turned to flame, my sinews to blazing fire, my bones to juniper coals, my eyelashes to lightning flashes, my eyeballs to fiery torches, the hairs of my head to hot flames, all my limbs to wings of burning fire, and the substance of my body to blazing fire."[4]

---

[3] Philip Alexander, "3 (Hebrew Apocalypse of) Enoch," in *The Old Testament Pseudepigrapha*, ed., J.H. Charlesworth (New York: Doubleday, 1985), 1.256.

[4] 3 Enoch 15 (Synopse 19) Philip Alexander, "3 (Hebrew Apocalypse of) Enoch," in *The Old Testament Pseudepigrapha*, ed., J.H. Charlesworth (New York: Doubleday, 1985), 267. See Revelation 1:13-15.

Enoch's unique transformation allows him to stand before God's presence in a manner that no other angel can. 2 Enoch 21:1-3 states:

> "*I saw the view of the face of the Lord*, like iron, made burning hot in a fire [and] brought out, and it emits sparks and is incandescent. Thus even I *saw the face of the Lord*. But the face of the Lord is not to be talked about, it is so very marvelous and supremely awesome and supremely frightening. [And] who am I to give an account of the incomprehensible being of the Lord, and of his face, so extremely strange and indescribable. And I remained alone at the end of the seventh heaven and became afraid, and fell on my face and said to myself: Woe is me, what has befallen me?"[5]

The *Hekhalot Zutarti*[6] relates that "when the youth [Enoch-Metatron] enters below the throne of glory, God

---

[5] 2 Enoch 22:6 states: "And who am I to tell of the Lord's unspeakable being, and of his very wonderful face? And I cannot tell the quantity of his many instructions, and various voices, the Lord's throne (is) very great and not made with hands, nor the quantity of those standing round him, troops of Cherubim and seraphim, nor their incessant singing, nor his immutable beauty, and who shall tell of the ineffable greatness of his glory." 2 Enoch 67:2 also highlights the permanency of Enoch's elevation. "And the angels hurried and grasped Enoch and carried him up to the highest heaven, where the Lord received him and made him stand in front of his face for eternity." Anderson "2 Enoch" 194.

[6] *Hekhalot Zutarti* is likely one of the oldest hekhalot texts. Ithamar Gruenwald, "Hekhalot Zutarti in Apocalyptic and

embraces him with a shining face…"⁷ Metatron is not harmed before God's presence, unlike the other angels who must protect their faces from the direct sight of God. 2 Enoch 39 states:

> "1 Oh my children, my beloved ones, hear the admonition of your father, as much as is according to the Lord's will. 2 I have been let come to you today, and announce to you, not from my lips, but from the Lord's lips, all that is and was and all that is now, and all that will be till judgment-day.
>
> 3 For the Lord has let me come to you, you hear, therefore, the words of my lips, of a man-made big for you, but I am one *who has seen the Lord's face*, like iron made to glow from fire it sends forth sparks and burns. 4 You look now upon my eyes, (the eyes) of a man big with meaning for you, but I have seen the Lord's eyes, shining like the sun's rays and filling the eyes of man with awe.
>
> 5 You see now, my children, the right hand of a man that helps you, but I have seen the Lord's right hand filling heaven as he helped me. 6 You see the compass of my work like your own, but I have seen the Lord's limitless and perfect compass, which has no end."

Merkavah Mysticism," Ancient Judaism and Early Christianity, Volume: 90 (2014): 176.

⁷ Synopse 385. See Andrei A. Orlov, *From Patriarch to the Youth: The Metatron Tradition in 2 Enoch*, PhD diss. (Milwaukee: Marquette University, 2004), 166.

Metatron withstands because he is *Sar haPanim*.[8] Enoch-Metatron's unique role is the reason for caution. His access to the area of the throne of glory warrants a warning.

> "Now, see the youth, who is going forth to meet you from the behind the throne of glory. Do not bow down to him, because his crown is like the crown of his King…and the robe on him is like the robe of his king."[9]

---

[8] I Enoch 38:4 states: "From that time those that possess the earth shall no longer be powerful and exalted: And they shall not be able to behold the face of the holy, For the Lord of Spirits has caused His light to appear On the face of the holy, righteous, and elect."

[9] Cairo Genizah Peter Schafer, ed., *Synopse Zur Hekhalot-Literatur* (Tübingen: Mohr Siebeck, 1991), 162-163. Jarl Fossum comments that "as part of his installation as God's vice-regent in heave, Enoch is given new clothes…a robe of honor on which were fixed all kinds of beauty, splendor, brilliance, and majesty. Jarl Fossum, "Ascensio, Metamorphosis: The 'Transfiguration' of Jesus in the Synoptic Gospels," in *The Image of the invisible God: Essays on the Influence of Jewish Mysticism on Early Christology* (Gottingen: Vandenhoeck & Ruprecht, 1995), 71-94. In a similar vein, Christopher Morray-Jones notes that Metatron "sites on the throne which is a replica of the Throne of Glory and wears a glorious robe like that of God. He functions as the agent of God in the creation, acts as intermediary between heavenly and lower worlds…" Christopher Morray-Jones, "Transformational mysticism in the Apocalyptic-Merkabah tradition," Journal of Jewish Studies 43, 1 (1992):8.

This cautionary word is noted by scholars who have analyzed the intimacy of Metatron with the Divine Presence. Nathaniel Deutsch comments:

> "Some sources understood Metatron to be the hypostatic embodiment of a particular part of the divine form, most notably the face of God[10]...it is likely that this tradition underlies the title *sar ha-panim*, which is associated with Metatron. Rather than 'prince of the face [of God], 'this title is better understood as 'prince who is the face [of God].'"[11]

Despite his unique position in the heavenly court, *Sefer Hekhalot* notes that Metatron's authority was less than YHWH's eight princes. However, his authority was above all other princes.[12] The revelation of the Torah at Sinai is even credited to Enoch. He is the Prince of the Torah. *Sefer Hekhalot* relates:

---

[10] See Colossians 1:15.

[11] Nathaniel Deutsch, *Guardians of the Gate: Angelic Vice Regency in Late Antiquity* (Boston: Brill, 1998), 43. Deutsch notes the passage that states, "Moses said to the Lord of all the worlds: 'If your face does not go [with us], do not bring me up from here.' [Exodus 33:15] The Lord of all the worlds warned Moses that he should beware of that face of his. So it is written, 'Beware of his face.' [Exodus 23:2] This is he who is written with the one letter by which heaven and earth were created, and was sealed with the seal of 'I am that I am' [Exodus 3:14]...This is the prince who is called Yofiel Yadariel...he is called Metatron. [Synopse 396-397]. Nathaniel Deutsch, *Guardians of the Gate: Angelic Vice Regency in Late Antiquity* (Boston: Brill, 1998), 43.

[12] 3 Enoch 10:3.

"Metatron brought it [Torah] out from my storehouses and committed it to Moses, and Moses to Joshua, Joshua to the Elders, the Elders to the Prophets, the Prophets to the Men of the Great Synagogue, the Men of the Great Synagogue to Ezra the Scribe, Ezra the Scribe to Hillel, the Elder, Hillel the Elder to Rabbi Abbahu, Rabbi Abbahu to Rabbi Zira, Rabbi Zira to the Men of Faith, and the Men of Faith to the Faithful..."[13]

---

[13] Synopse 80. Philip Alexander, "3 (Hebrew Apocalypse of) Enoch," in The Old Testament Pseudepigrapha, ed., J.H. Charlesworth (New York: Doubleday, 1985), 315.

CHAPTER 8

Enoch as the Prince of the World

Enoch-Metatron also holds another unique title. He was designated as the Prince of the World. The title is likely connected to Adam's original place in the created order. 2 Enoch 58:2-5 states:

> "2 In those days when the Lord came down on to earth for Adam's sake, and visited all his creatures, which he created himself, after all these he created Adam, and the Lord called all the beasts of the earth, all the reptiles, and all the birds that soar in the air, and brought them all before the face of our father, Adam.
>
> 3 And Adam gave the names to all things living on earth.
>
> 4 And *the Lord appointed him ruler over all*, and subjected to him all things under his hands[1], and made them dumb and made them dull that they be

---

[1] See I Corinthians 8:6; Ephesians 1:21.

commanded of man, and be in subjection and obedience to him.

5 Thus, also the Lord created every man lord over all his possessions."[2]

The shorter recension of 2 Enoch first portrays Enoch in this role. In the following passage, Enoch relates his newly found status in heaven to his earthly children.

"And behold my children, I am the Governor of the earth. I wrote (them) down. And the whole year I combined, and the hours of the day. And the hours I measured; and I wrote down every seed on earth. And I compared every measure and the just balance I measured. And I wrote (them) down, just as the Lord commanded…I the doings of each person will put down, and no one will

---

[2] This view appears as early as Philo of Alexandria. "And, as was very natural, the power of domination was excessive in that first-created man, whom God formed with great care and thought worthy of the second rank in the creation, *making him his own viceroy and the ruler of all other creatures*. Since even those who have been born so many generations afterwards, when the race is becoming weakened by reason of the long intervals of time that have elapsed since the beginning of the world, do still exert the same power over the irrational beasts, preserving as it were a spark of the dominion and power which has been handed down to them by succession from their first ancestor." Philo, *On Creation*, LII. (148).

hide; because the Lord is the one who pays, and he will be the avenger on the judgment day."³

Sefer Hekhalot refers to the seventy-two princes of the kingdoms of the world.

"Whenever the Great Law Court sits in the height of the heaven *Arabot*, only the great princes who are called YHWH by the name of the Holy One, blessed be he, are permitted to speak. How many princes are there? There are 72 princes of kingdoms in the world, not counting the Prince of the World, who speaks in favor of the world before the Holy One, blessed be he, every day at the hour when the book is opened in which every deed in the world is recorded, as it is written, 'A court was held, and the books were opened.'"⁴

---

³ Francis Andersen, "2 (Slavonic Apocalypse of) Enoch," in *The Old Testament Pseudepigrapha*, ed. J.H. Charlesworth (New York: Doubleday, 1985), 217-219.

⁴ Philip Alexander, "3 (Hebrew Apocalypse of) Enoch," in *The Old Testament Pseudepigrapha*, ed., J.H. Charlesworth (New York: Doubleday, 1985), 285. Peter Schafer, ed., *Synopse Zur Hekhalot-Literatur* (Tübingen: Mohr Siebeck, 1991), 24-25. Philo of Alexandria includes a passage in his works which provides additional insight into the idea of divine measurement. "And 'Gomorra' [means] 'measure' true and just is the Divine Logos, by which have been measured and are measured all things that are on earth-principles, numbers and proportions in harmony and consonance being included, through which the form and measures of existing things are seen." R. Marcus, trans., *Philo, Questions and Answers on Genesis* (Cambridge: Harvard University Press, 1949), 296-297.

In the *Pirkei de-Rabbi Eliezer 27*, the archangel Michael is given the title Prince of the world. For Gershom Scholem, the traditions about Michael and Metatron may have equally enhanced each folklore.[5]

---

[5] Gershom G. Scholem, *Jewish Gnosticism, Merkabah Mysticism, and Talmudic Tradition* (New York: Jewish Theological Seminary of America, 1960), 48.

CHAPTER 9

Enoch as the Lesser Deity

The elevation of Enoch-Metatron to the Prince of the face and the Prince of the World may have set the stage for a natural progression to the most significant and theologically challenging title given to the exalted patriarch. Andrei Orlov compares Enoch-Metatron and considers the original founding character that Enoch is associated with, Enmeduranki.

> "In *Sefer Hekhalot*, however, when Enoch is elevated above the angelic world and brought into the immediate presence of the Deity, the traditional divinatory techniques have become unnecessary since the hero himself is now situated not outside but inside the divine realm and becomes a kind of a second, junior deity, considered as the lesser manifestation of God's name."[1]

---

[1] Andrei A. Orlov, *From Patriarch to the Youth: The Metatron Tradition in 2 Enoch,* PhD diss. (Milwaukee: Marquette University, 2004), 50.

Sefer Hekhalot or 3 Enoch is referred to three times as the *YHWH Hakatan,* the little or lesser Hashem.[2] In 3 Enoch 12, Enoch-Metatron relates to Rabbi Ishmael that God has proclaimed him as follows:

> "The Holy One, blessed be he, fashioned for me a majestic robe…and he called me, 'The Lesser YHWH' in the presence of his whole household in the height, as it is written, 'My name is in him.'"[3]

The designation of Enoch-Metatron by this name is without question the most challenging premise to the emerging rabbinic class that at least in the Talmud had rejected the possibility of multiple powers in heaven. Alternatively, Talmudic objections may be based on complete equivalency between the powers.[4] The Bavli Sanhedrin 38b relates:

> "Rabbi Nahman said: He who is as skilled in refuting the Minim as is Rabbi Idith, let him do so; but not otherwise. Once a Min said to Rabbi Idith: It is written, And unto Moses He said,

---

[2] See 3 Enoch 12:2, 48C:7; 48D:1 [90]. Ibid., 184.

[3] Synopse 15. Philip Alexander, "3 (Hebrew Apocalypse of) Enoch," in *The Old Testament Pseudepigrapha*, ed., J.H. Charlesworth (New York: Doubleday, 1985), 265.

[4] Alan Segal comments that "in the Hebrew Book of Enoch, Metatron is set on a throne alongside God and appointed above angels and powers to function as God's vizir and plenipotentiary." Alan F. Segal, *Two Powers in Heaven: Early Rabbinic Reports about Christianity and Gnosticism* (Waco: Baylor University Press, 2012), 63.

Come up to the Lord. But surely it should have stated, Come up unto me! — It was Metatron [who said that], he replied, whose name is similar to that of his Master, for it is written, For my name is in him. But if so, [he retorted,] we should worship him! The same passage, however, — replied Rabbi Idith says: Be not rebellious against him, i.e., exchange Me not for him. But if so, why is it stated: He will not pardon your transgression? He answered: By our truth, we would not accept him even as a messenger, for it is written, And he said unto him, If Thy [personal] presence go not, etc.

A Min once said to Rabbi Ishmael b. Jose: It is written, Then the Lord caused to rain upon Sodom and Gomorrah brimstone and fire from the Lord: but from him should have been written! A certain fuller said, Leave him to me, I will answer him. [He then proceeded,' It is written, And Lamech said to his wives, Ada and Zillah, Hear my voice, ye wives of Lamech; but he should have said, my wives! But such is the Scriptural idiom — so here too, it is the Scriptural idiom."[5]

Commenting on 3 Enoch 12 and 48C, Hugo Odeberg notes the following regarding the title Lesser Hashem. Hugo Odeberg notes it,

---

[5] Isidore Epstein, *The Babylonian Talmud* (London: Soncino Press, 1984).

> "as indicative of Metatron's character of representative, vicarious, of the Godhead; it expresses a sublimation of his vice-regency into a second manifestation of the Deity in the name YHWH."[6]

In the designation of Enoch-Metatron as the lesser Hashem, there is an amalgamation of many roles and functions which evolved from the earliest strata of the Enoch tradition. Christopher Morray-Jones comments on this by noting that,

> "As the Angel of the LORD, Metatron functions as the celestial vice-regent who ministers before the Throne, supervises the celestial liturgy and officiates over the heavenly hosts. *He sits on the throne which is a replica of the Throne of Glory and wears a glorious robe like that of God.* He functions as the agent of God in the creation, acts as an intermediary between heavenly and lower worlds, is the guide of the ascending visionary, and reveals the celestial secrets to mankind. He is, by delegating divine authority, the rule and the judge of the world. He is thus a *Logos* figure and an embodiment of the divine Glory. In his *shi'ur qomah*, we are told that Metatron's body, like the *kabod*, fills the entire world, though the writer is

---

[6] Hugo Odeberg, *3 Enoch*, 1.82. J. Fr. Von Meyer stated, "…the Jewish conception of Metatron forms an exact counterpart of the Christian conception of the Son of God, [and] hence points to Revelation 3:21 as a parallel." Ibid., 136.

careful to maintain a distinction between Metatron and the Glory of God Himself."[7]

The description of Metatron's body is perhaps reminiscent of the Talmud's description of Adam's body. The Bavli Sanhedrin 38b states:

> "Rabbi Judah said in the name of Rav: Adam's body reached from one end of the world to the other. But after he acted offensively, the Holy One laid His hand upon him and diminished him, as is said, 'Thou hast hemmed me in behind and before, so that Thou was able to lay Thy hand upon me. (Psalm 139:5)."

The *Apocalypse of Abraham,* a pseudepigraphic work possibly written during the late first or second century CE, also contains a description of Adam's giant body. 23:4-6 states:

> "And I looked into the picture, and my eyes ran to the side of the Garden of Eden, and I saw there a man very great in height and terrible in breadth, incomparable in aspect, entwined with a woman who was also equal to the man in aspect and size. And they were standing under the tree of Eden."

The contrast between Adam and Metatron is crucial because it lays the foundation for the idea that Enoch, with this transformation into Metatron, rectified Adam's

---

[7] Christopher Morray-Jones, "Transformational mysticism in the Apocalyptic-Merkabah tradition," Journal of Jewish Studies 43, 1 (1992):8.

fall.⁸ A little known Armenian text titled *The Words of Adam and Seth* conveys the following tradition.

> "But he [Adam], not having observed the commandments, and having been stripped of the divine light, and having been thrown outside the Garden, became an equal of the dumb beast. And Enoch considered these things, and for forty days and for forty nights he did not eat at all.⁹ And after this, he planted in it fruit bears, and he was in the garden four hundred and forty-two years, and after that, in body, *he was taken up heaven, and was found worthy of the divine glory and light.*"¹⁰

Sefer Hekhalot describes Enoch-Metatron as God's vice-regent. Enoch-Metatron is exalted above all other angels, except the eight princes of the LORD. *Sefer Hekhalot* 10:2-6 states:

---

⁸ Philip Alexander notes, "behind these passages is a concept of Metatron as a divine entity first incarnate in Adam and then reincarnate in Enoch. Enoch, having perfected himself, in contrast to Adam, who sinned and fell, re-ascends to his heavenly home and takes his rightful place in the heights of the universe, above the highest angels...Enoch thus becomes a redeemer figure-a second Adam through whom humanity is restored." Philip Alexander, "From Son of Adam to a Second God: Transformation of the Biblical Enoch," in *Biblical Figures Outside the Bible*, ed. M. Stone and T. Bergen (Harrisburg: Trinity Press, 1998), 111.

⁹ Mark 4:1-11; Matthew 4:2.

¹⁰ Michael E. Stone, *Armenian Apocrypha Relating to the Patriarchs and Prophets* (Jerusalem: Israel Academy of Sciences and Humanities 1982), 12-13.

"He [God] placed it [the throne] at the door of the seventh palace and sat me down upon it. And the herald went out into every heaven and announced concerning me: 'I have appointed Metatron my servant as the prince and a ruler over all the denizens of the heights, apart from the eight great, honored, and terrible princes who are called YHWH by the name of their King.[11] Any angel and any prince who has anything to say in my presence should go before him and speak to him. Whatever he says to you in my name you must observe and do, because I have committed to him the Prince of Wisdom and the Prince of Understanding, to teach him the wisdom of those above and of those below, the wisdom of this

---

[11] Alan F. Segal comments that "a principal angel was seen as God's primary or sole helper and allowed to share in God's divinity. That a human being, as the hero or exemplar of a particular group, could ascend to become one with this figure- as Enoch, Moses or Elijah had-seems also to have been part of the tradition." *Two Powers in Heaven: Early Rabbinic Reports about Christianity and Gnosticism* (Waco: Baylor University Press, 2012), 180. Regarding the inherent theological challenges associated with two powers in heaven, Daniel Boyarin states: "Moreover, in some of the best work on the use of heresiology to produce orthodoxy among Christians, it has been shown that almost always the so-called 'heresy' is not a new invader from outside but an integral and usually more ancient version of the religious tradition that is now being displaced by a newer set of conceptions, portraying the relations almost mystifyingly in the direct opposite of the observed chronologies." Daniel Boyarin, "Beyond Judaisms: Metatron and the Divine Polymorphy of Ancient Judaism," Journal for the Study of Judaism 41 (2010):325.

world and of the world to come. Moreover, I have put in charge of all the stores of the palaces of Arabot, and all the treasures that are in heavenly heights.'"[12]

Shi'ur Qomah, i.e., the measure of the Divine body, is part of the Hekhalot literature. It chronicles the names and dimensions of God's physical limbs. The text's preponderance consists of teachings that Metatron revealed to the Tanna, Rabbi Ishmael, who conveyed it to his students and Rabbi Akiba. The text survives in fragmented form. Its date of origin has been debated.[13] Gershom Scholem believed that it was from,

"either the Tannaitic or the early Amoraic period."[14]

---

[12] Philip Alexander, "3 (Hebrew Apocalypse of) Enoch," in *The Old Testament Pseudepigrapha*, ed., J.H. Charlesworth (New York: Doubleday, 1985), 264.

[13] Philip Alexander opines that, "…we can posit, therefore, c.A.D. 450 as a reasonably firm terminus post quem for the emergence of the full-blown Enoch-Metatron of 3 Enoch, though we must bear in mind that he marks the culmination of a process of evolution which began in Maccabean times, if not earlier." Philip Alexander, "The Historical Settings of the Hebrew Book of Enoch," JJS 28 (1977): 164-165.

[14] Gershom Scholem, "Jewish Gnosticism, Merkabah Mysticism, and Talmudic Tradition: Based on the Israel Goldstein lectures," delivered at the Jewish Theological Seminary of America, New York. Edition: 2. Published by Jewish Theological Seminary of America, 1965), 40.

Rabbi Moses ben Maimon considered it a counterfeit.[15] He also believed that it was heretical and should be burned.[16] Not all rabbis of Iberian origin were opposed to the text. Rabbi Moses Narboni also authored a philosophic work titled *Iggeret Al-Shi'ur Qomah*. In it, Rabbi Narboni dismissed the obvious anthropomorphisms of *Shi'ur Qomah* as speaking figuratively.[17]

The differences between Enoch-Metatron and Enmeduranki become more significant as the Enoch tradition developed. As Andrei Orlov notes,

---

[15] Shlomo Pines and Yirmiahu Yovel, *Maimonides and Philosophy: Papers Presented at the Sixth Jerusalem Philosophical Encounter* (Boston: M. Nijhoff Publishers, 1985), footnote 11, relying on J. Blau, R. Moses B. Maimon — Responsa (Jerusalem, 1958), 1:201.

[16] Shlomo Pines and Yirmiahu Yovel, *Maimonides and Philosophy: Papers Presented at the Sixth Jerusalem Philosophical Encounter* (Boston: M. Nijhoff Publishers, 1985), 85.

[17] Colette Sirat, A History of Jewish Philosophy in the Middle Ages (Cambridge: Cambridge University Press, 1990), 334. The importance of the text, at least as purported by the text itself is conveyed by the following quote: "Rabbi Ishmael said: When I said this thing before Rabbi Akiva, he said to me: Whoever knows the measure of the height (shi'ur qomah) of the Creator and the praise of the Holy Blessed One is protected from all creatures, secure in being a child of the world-to-come, and they will lengthen his days. Rabbi Ishmael said: Akiva and I are guarantors in this matter, but only if one recites this mishnah each day." This view may enhance speculation that Shi'ur Qomah began as a commentary on the Song of Songs and the classical rabbinic view that this book is an allegory of love between God and the people of Israel. Translation of British Library ms.10675, in Martin Samuel Cohen, *The Shi'ur Qomah: Texts and Recensions* (Tubingen: Mohr Siebeck, 1985),192-194.

Enmeduranki entered the heavenly court temporarily.[18] Enoch's ascension and transformation to Metatron also entailed the assumption of other characteristics that linked Enoch-Metatron to God. Enoch-Metatron's transformation included the deboublement or duplication of the divine body or at least an aspect of it. *Sefer Hekhalot* relates this transformation.

> "I was enlarged and increased in size till I matched the world in length and breath. He made to grown on me 72 wings, 36 on one side and 36 on the other, and each single wing covered the entire world..."[19]

Andrei Orlov emphasizes Enoch-Metatron's roles, which refer to the latter as the Measurer of the Lord and the possessor of the body. These responsibilities are coupled with his actions as *Sar happanim*.[20] In *Sefer Hekhalot*[21] and *Shi'ur Qomah,* the various elements of Metatron's roles are brought together.

> "I increased his stature by seventy thousand parasangs, above very every height, among those

---

[18] Andrei A. Orlov, *From Patriarch to the Youth: The Metatron Tradition in 2 Enoch,* PhD diss. (Milwaukee: Marquette University, 2004), 186.

[19] Philip Alexander, "3 (Hebrew Apocalypse of) Enoch," in *The Old Testament Pseudepigrapha,* ed., J.H. Charlesworth (New York: Doubleday, 1985), 263.

[20] Andrei A. Orlov, *From Patriarch to the Youth: The Metatron Tradition in 2 Enoch,* PhD diss. (Milwaukee: Marquette University, 2004), 194.

[21] 3 Enoch 48C:5-6.

who are tall of stature. I magnified his throne from the majesty of my throne. I increased his honor from the glory of my honor. I turned his flesh to fiery torches and all the hones of his body to coals of light. I made the appearance of his eyes like the appearance of lightning and the light of his eyes like 'light unfailing.' I caused his face to shine like the brilliant light of the sun."[22]

Genesis Rabbah 8:1 similarly describes Adam's body, adding to the view that Enoch-Metatron reflects Adam before his disobedience.

"Rabbi Tanhuma in the name of Rabbi Banayah and Rabbi Berekiah in the name of Rabbi Eleazar said: He created him [Adam] as a lifeless mass extending from one end of the world to the other; thus it is written, 'Thine .eyes did not see mine unformed substance (Psalm 139:16).' Rabbi Joshua ben Rabbi Nehemiah and Rabbi Judah ben Rabbi Simon in Rabbi Eleazar's name said: 'He created him filling the whole world. How do we know [that he stretched] from east to west? Because it is said, "Thou has formed behind...and before...' From north to south? Because it says, 'since the day that God created man upon the earth, and from the one end of heaven unto the other (Deuteronomy 4:32). And how do we know

---

[22] Philip Alexander, "3 (Hebrew Apocalypse of) Enoch," in *The Old Testament Pseudepigrapha*, ed., J.H. Charlesworth (New York: Doubleday, 1985), 312. Peter Schafer, ed., *Synopse Zur Hekhalot-Literatur* (Tübingen: Mohr Siebeck, 1991), 36-37.

that he filled the empty spaces of the world? From the verse, 'And laid Thy hand upon me' (as you read, Withdraw Thy hand from me. (Job 13:21)."[23]

A passage from *Pirke de-Rabbi Eliezer* also comments on the expansiveness of Adam's body. Still, it highlights an issue of particular importance to the relationship of Enoch-Metatron to God. *Pirke de-Rabbi Eliezer 11* states:

> "He [God] began to collect the dust of the first man from the four corners of the world...He [Adam] stood upon his feet, and was in the likeness of God; his height extended from the east to the west, as it is said, 'Behind and in from Thou has formed me.' Behind, that is the west, and in front, that is the east. All creatures saw him and were afraid of him; they thought he was their creator, and prostrated themselves before him."[24]

The confusion about Adam was not limited to the animals. The angels also were confused because God created man in His image. *Genesis Rabbah* 8:10 explains that,

> "The ministering angels mistook him [for a divine being] and wished to exclaim 'Holy' before Him...what did the Holy One, blessed be He, do?

---

[23] See also Genesis Rabbah 21:3; 24:2.
[24] *Pirke de Rabbi Eliezer*, tr. G. Friedlander (New York: Hermon Press, 1965), 76-79.

He caused sleep to fall upon him, and so all knew that he was [only a mortal] man."[25]

Despite the aggrandizement of Enoch-Metatron with a divine body, a distinction is retained between Metatron and God.[26] Nevertheless, the connection between Metatron and God is clear. Joseph Dan notes that Metatron,

---

[25] The little known work titled *Alphabet of Rabbi Akiba* also states: "This teaches that initially Adam was created from the earth to the firmament. When the ministering angels saw him, they were shocked and excited by him. At that time, they all stood before the Holy One, blessed be H, and said to Him; 'Master of the Universe! There are two powers in the world, one in heaven and one on earth.' What did the Holy One, blessed be He, do then? He placed His hand on him, and decreased him, setting him at one thousand cubits." Moshe Idel, "Enoch is Metatron," Immanuel 24/25 (1990): 226.

[26] Martin Cohen also notes the distinctions between God and Metatron. Cohen states, "whereas the sole of foot or the pinky-finger of the Deity is said to be one universe-length long, Metatron himself is altogether only that height." Martin S. Cohen, *Shiur Qomah: Liturgy and Theurgy in Pre-Kabbalistic Jewish Mysticism* (New York: University Press Of America, 1983), 133. Against this, Andrei Orlov posits, "These distinctions, however should not be overestimated since they do not prevent the Shi'ur Qomah materials from unifying both corporealities through and identical terminology. In the Merkabah materials the divine corporeality is labeled the Stature/Measure of the Body. The same terminology is often applied to Enoch-Metatron's body." Andrei A. Orlov, *From Patriarch to the Youth: The Metatron Tradition in 2 Enoch,* PhD diss. (Milwaukee: Marquette University, 2004), 193.

"...sits on the throne of glory, he has spread over himself a canopy of radiance, such as the one over the Throne of Glory itself, and his throne is placed at the entrance to the seventh *hekhal*, in which stands the Throne of Glory of God Himself. Metatron sits on it as God sits on His Throne."[27]

Sefer Hekhalot appears to convey the idea that Metatron was first incarnated in Adam[28] and then in Enoch.[29]

(1) Aleph I made him strong, I took him, I appointed him: (namely) Metatron, my servant who is one (unique) among all the children of heaven. I made him strong in the generation of the first Adam. But when I beheld the men of the generation of the flood, that they were corrupt, then I went and removed my Shekina from among them. And 1 lifted it up on high with the sound of a trumpet and with a shout, as it is written (Ps.xlvii.

---

[27] Joseph Dan, *The Ancient Jewish Mysticism* (Tel Aviv, MOD Books, 1993), 115-117.

[28] 3 Enoch 48C:1 (Synopse 72) states: "The Holy One, blessed be he, said: I made him strong, I took him, I appointed him, namely Metatron my servant, who is unique among all the denizens of the heights...'I made him strong' in the generation of the first man..." Philip Alexander, "3 (Hebrew Apocalypse of) Enoch," in *The Old Testament Pseudepigrapha*, ed., J.H. Charlesworth (New York: Doubleday, 1985), 311.

[29] Andrei A. Orlov, *From Patriarch to the Youth: The Metatron Tradition in 2 Enoch,* PhD diss. (Milwaukee: Marquette University, 2004), 146.

6): 'God is gone up with a shout, the Lord with the sound of a trumpet.'"[30]

Philip Alexander interprets the significance of this passage.

"Enoch thus becomes a redeemer figure- a second Adam through whom humanity is restored."[31]

This passage is striking since it is quite similar to the claims made about Jesus of Nazareth. While Enoch's imagery is incredibly similar to the redemptive work attributed to Jesus, there is a problem as Francis Andersen notes that this view "could hardly please a Christian or a Jew."[32]

---

[30] Chapter XL VIII Alternate Version; 3 Enoch 48C:1 (Synopse 72).

[31] Philip Alexander, "From Son of Adam to a Second God: Transformation of the Biblical Enoch," in *Biblical Figures Outside the Bible*, ed. M. Stone and T. Bergen (Harrisburg, Penn.: Trinity Press, 1998), 111.

[32] Francis Andersen, "2 (Slavonic Apocalypse of) Enoch," in *The Old Testament Pseudepigrapha*, ed. J.H. Charlesworth (New York: Doubleday, 1985), 190.

CHAPTER 10

Enoch as Mediator

The idea of Enoch as a mediator is a critical element of Enochic literature. Andrei Orlov explains the role of Enoch as a mediator. Orlov notes that "Enoch can be seen as a figure able to successfully mediate knowledge and judgment, acting not only as an intercessor and petitioner for the creatures of the lower realm but also as a special envoy of the Deity responsible for bringing the woes and condemnations to the sinful creatures of the earth."[1]

Here, Enoch's first unlikely role as ``mediator begins.[2] Although he is a human being, Enoch is asked to serve as an intermediary for the fallen angelic group, i.e., the *Fallen Watchers*. Enoch's role as a mediator grew

---

[1] Andrei A. Orlov, *From Patriarch to the Youth: The Metatron Tradition in 2 Enoch,* PhD diss. (Milwaukee: Marquette University, 2004), 140.

[2] 2 Enoch [Longer recension, ms. J] (tr. Francis Andersen). https://goo.gl/o5JuJi. The significance of this is not lost when Philip Alexander states: "Enoch has become a redeemer figure- a second Adam who humanity is restored."

significantly. In 2 Enoch 64, he is designated as having taken away the sins of the world in a manner derived from Isaiah 53.

> "And when Enoch had spoken |these words| to his sons and to the princes of the people, and all his people, near and far, having heard that the LORD was calling Enoch, they consulted one another, saying, "Let us go, let us kiss Enoch." And they came together, up to 2000 men, and they arrived at the place Akhuzan where Enoch was, and his sons. And the elders of the people and all the community came and prostrated themselves and kissed Enoch. And they said to him, 'O our father, Enoch! May you be blessed by the LORD, the eternal king! And now, bless your 〈|sons|〉, and all the people, so that we may be glorified in front of your face today. For you will be glorified in front of the face 〈|of the LORD for eternity|〉, because you are the one whom the LORD chose in preference to all the people upon the earth; and he appointed you to be the one who makes a written record of all his creation, visible and invisible, **and the one who carried away the sin of mankind** and the helper of your own household.' And Enoch answered his people, saying to all of them."[3]

---

[3] James C. Vanderkam, *Enoch: A Man for All Generations* (Columbia: University of South Carolina, 1995), 28.

Andrei Orlov points to a clear difference between Enmeduranki and Enoch.

> "In contrast to the king of Sippar, whose mediation involves the task of bringing celestial knowledge to humans, the seventh antediluvian patriarch is portrayed as the one who not only dispatches knowledge from the celestial to the terrestrial realm but also conveys messages received in the lower realms to God and other celestial beings."[4]

Andrei Orlov believes that Enoch's role as mediator became the basis for his eventual transformation into Metatron and the Prince of the World.[5] Orlov states:

> "Enoch has already accomplished his role as the redeemer of humanity through his luminous metamorphosis near the throne of glory. Humanity has been redeemed in him, and this redemption gives hope to other righteous ones, who will later attain the paradisal condition. The significant detail that confirms Enoch's unique redeeming role is that unlike in Chapter 53, where he opposed the idea of intercession, in 2 Enoch 64-65,

---

[4] Andrei A. Orlov, *From Patriarch to the Youth: The Metatron Tradition in 2 Enoch,* PhD diss. (Milwaukee: Marquette University, 2004), 77.

[5] Ibid., 77.

he does not object to the idea that he is able to carry away the sin of humanity."[6]

In a previously quoted section of 3 Enoch, Enoch, as Metatron, relates the extent of his insight into man's condition.

> "Rabbi Ishmael said: Metatron, the angel, the Prince of the Presence, said to me:
>
> (1) Henceforth the Holy One, blessed be He, revealed to me all the mysteries of Tora and all the secrets of wisdom and all the depths of the Perfect Law; and all living beings' thoughts of heart and all the secrets of the universe and all the secrets of Creation were revealed unto me even as they are revealed unto the Maker of Creation.
>
> (2) And I watched intently to behold the secrets of the depth and the wonderful mystery. Before a man did think in secret, I saw (it) and before a man made a thing, I beheld it.
>
> (3) And there was nothing on high nor in the deep hidden from me."[7]

The response of the fallen angels to Enoch's presence is particularly noteworthy. I Enoch 13:1-8 relates,

---

[6] Andrei A. Orlov, *From Patriarch to the Youth: The Metatron Tradition in 2 Enoch,* PhD diss. (Milwaukee: Marquette University, 2004), 308.

[7] 3 Enoch 11:1-3.

"1 And Enoch went and said: 'Azazel, thou shalt have no peace: a severe sentence has gone forth 2 against thee to put thee in bonds: And thou shalt not have toleration nor request granted to thee, because of the unrighteousness which thou hast taught, and because of all the works of godlessness 3 and unrighteousness and sin which thou hast shown to men.' Then I went and spoke to them all 4 together, and they were all afraid, and fear and trembling seized them. *And they besought me to draw up a petition for them that they might find forgiveness, and to read their petition in the presence 5 of the Lord of heaven.* For from thenceforward they could not speak (with Him) nor lift up their 6 eyes to heaven for shame of their sins for which they had been condemned. Then I wrote out their petition and the prayer in regard to their spirits and their deeds individually and in regard to their 7 requests that they should have forgiveness and length. And I went off and sat down at the waters of Dan, in the land of Dan, to the south of the west of Hermon: I read their petition till I fell 8 asleep. And behold a dream came to me, and visions fell down upon me, and I saw visions of chastisement, and a voice came bidding (me) I to tell it to the sons of heaven, and reprimand them."

Though Enoch is only a mortal, the fallen angels tremble with fear at his arrival.[8] As Vanderkam notes, the significance of this is clear.

> "Enoch clearly outranks these angels and is their superior in virtue. Enoch later sees in a vision that he should reprove the watchers, and this he does (13:7-10)."[9]

Enoch gives the fallen angels their judgment of eternal condemnation.[10] The fallen angels will not return to heaven. Their sons will be destroyed. The fallen angels will be bound until the Day of Judgment. In contrast to the heavenly Watchers who had lost their place in heaven, Enoch ascends to the God's throne room and stands in God's presence. Enoch describes the visionary

---

[8] The idea that Enoch was superior to the angels was accepted the early Church Father Irenaeus though his desire to invalidate the value of circumcision and hence ongoing Jewish identity becomes very clear. *Adversus Haereses 4.16.2* states: "Enoch too, pleasing God without circumcision, discharged the office of God's legate to the angels although he was a man, and was translated, and is preserved until now as a witness of the just judgment of God, because the angels when they had transgressed fell to the earth for judgment, but the man who pleased was translated [Him] for salvation. Annette Yoshiko Reed, *Fallen Angels and the History of Judaism and Christianity* (Cambridge: Cambridge Press, 2004), 158.

[9] James C. Vanderkam, *Enoch: A Man for All Generations* (Columbia: University of South Carolina, 1995), 29.

[10] The *Book of Jubilees* 4:22 relates: "And he testified to the Watchers, who had sinned with the daughters of men; for these had begun to unite themselves, so as to be defiled, with the daughters of men, and Enoch testified against (them) all.

journey he experienced. James Vanderkam notes that Enoch's description highlights an experience never claimed by other prophets or seers, including Isaiah, Ezekiel, or Daniel. While the former prophets saw the divine environs, Enoch ascends and sees the divine throne in God's celestial palace.[11]

> "And the vision was shown to me thus: Behold, in the vision clouds, invited me and a mist summoned me, and the course of the stars and the lightnings sped and hastened me, and the winds in 9 the vision caused me to fly and lifted me upward, and bore me into heaven. And I went in till I drew nigh to a wall which is built of crystals and surrounded by tongues of fire: and it began to affright 10 me. And I went into the tongues of fire and drew nigh to a large house which was built of crystals: and the walls of the house were like a tesselated floor (made) of crystals, and its groundwork was 11 of crystal. Its ceiling was like the path of the stars and the lightnings, and between them were 12 fiery cherubim, and their heaven was (clear as) water. A flaming fire surrounded the walls, and its 13 portals blazed with fire. And I entered into that house, and it was hot as fire and cold as ice: there 14 were no delights of life therein: fear covered me, and trembling got hold upon me. And as I quaked 15 and trembled, I fell upon my face. And I beheld a vision, And lo!

---

[11] James C. Vanderkam, *Enoch: A Man for All Generations* (Columbia: University of South Carolina, 1995), 47.

there was a second house, greater 16 than the former, and the entire portal stood open before me, and it was built of flames of fire. And in every respect, it so excelled in splendor and magnificence and extent that I cannot describe to 17 you its splendor and its extent. And its floor was of fire, and above it were lightnings and the path 18 of the stars, and its ceiling also was flaming fire. And I looked and saw therein a lofty throne: its appearance was as crystal, and the wheels thereof as the shining sun, and there was the vision of 19 cherubim. And from underneath the throne came streams of flaming fire so that I could not look 20 thereon. And the Great Glory sat thereon, and His raiment shone more brightly than the sun, and 21 was whiter than any snow."

Enoch is overwhelmed and trembled in fear. Countless angels attend God, though none of them come near. Enoch, however, is called to draw close. I Enoch states:

"And until then, I had a covering on my face, as I trembled. And the Lord called me with his own mouth and said to me: 'Come hither, Enoch, to my holy word.' And he lifted me up and brought me to the door. And I looked, with my face down.

And he answered me and said to me with this voice: 'Hear! Do not be afraid, Enoch, (you) righteous man and scribed of righteousness. Come hither and hear my voice. And go, say to the Watchers of heaven who sent you to petition on their behalf: 'You ought to petition on behalf of men, not men on behalf of you.'"[12]

The Watchers, in contrast, are now barred from doing so.[13] Amid humanity's decline and descent into corruption, Enoch is absent from this decay. I Enoch 12:1-6 relates,

> "1 Before these things, Enoch was hidden, and no one of the children of men knew where he was 2 hidden, and where he abode, and what had become of him. And his activities had to do with the Watchers, and his days were with the holy ones. 3 And I Enoch was blessing the Lord of majesty and the King of the ages, and lo! the Watchers 4 called me -Enoch the scribe- and said to me: 'Enoch, thou scribe of righteousness, go, declare to the

---

[12] I Enoch 14:24-15:2.

[13] Ibid., 29. Andrei Orlov states: "The important aspect here is that the Watchers are not only ashamed to approach the Deity, they also seem to have lost their ability to serve effectively as mediators even on their behalf. It is interesting to note that the text implies that under current conditions even the faithful Watchers of heaven are not able to serve as mediators between God and their formers colleagues in the lower realm." Andrei A. Orlov, *From Patriarch to the Youth: The Metatron Tradition in 2 Enoch,* PhD diss. (Milwaukee: Marquette University, 2004), 87. James Vanderkam cites Enoch's uniqueness when he observes that, "Enoch, like the sinful angels, was one who crossed boundaries, but he, unlike them, retained the ability to retrace his steps. The angels, once they had committed themselves to the life of flesh and blood, lost the ability to return." James C. Vanderkam, *Enoch: A Man for All Generations* (Columbia: University of South Carolina, 1995), 88.

Watchers of the heaven who have left the high heaven, the holy eternal place, and have defiled themselves with women, and have done as the children of earth do, and have taken unto themselves 5 wives: "Ye have wrought great destruction on the earth: And ye shall have no peace nor forgiveness 6 of sin: and inasmuch as they delight themselves in their children, The murder of their beloved ones shall they see, and over the destruction of their children shall they lament and shall make supplication unto eternity, but mercy and peace shall ye not attain."[14]

The fallen angels' offspring, the giants, will die, but their impact on the world will continue.[15] The spirits of the giants will rise like ghosts from their bodies. They will continue to wreak havoc on humanity.[16] The fallen

---

[14] Andrei Orlov notes, "The Patriarch's scribal honorifics never appear as Enoch's self-designation, but always some from the mouth of various clients who benefits from the fruits of his scribal expertise." Andrei A. Orlov, *From Patriarch to the Youth: The Metatron Tradition in 2 Enoch,* PhD diss. (Milwaukee: Marquette University, 2004), 70.

[15] Baruch 3:26-29 reads, "26 There were the giants famous from the beginning, that were of so great stature, and so expert in war.27 Those did not the Lord choose, neither gave he the way of knowledge unto them: 28 But they were destroyed, because they had no wisdom, and perished through their own foolishness.29 Who hath gone up into heaven, and taken her, and brought her down from the clouds?"

[16] The Midrash of Semhazai and Azael relates, "Forthwith Metatron sent a messenger to Semhazai, and said to him; 'The Holy One is about to destroy His world, and bring it upon a flood.' Semhazai stood up and raises his voice and wept aloud, for he

angels and their wives are destined for punishment. I Enoch 19 relates a contradiction with an earlier section in the text. Earlier, the fallen angels were imprisoned; now, at least of the angels remain free to continue deceiving men.[17]

> "1 And Uriel said to me: 'Here shall stand the angels who have connected themselves with women, and their spirits assuming many different forms are defiling mankind and shall lead them astray into sacrificing to demons as gods, (here shall they stand,) till the day of the great judgment in 2 which they shall be judged till they are made an end of. And the women also of the angels who 3 went astray shall become sirens.'[18] And I,

was sorely troubled about his sons and (his own) iniquity. And he said: 'How shall my children live and what shall become of my children, for each one of them eats daily a thousand camels, a thousand horses, a thousand oxen, and all kinds (of animals)?" J. T. Milik, *The Books of Enoch: Aramaic fragments of Qumrân Cave 4* (Oxford: Clarendon Press, 1976), 328.

[17] The *Book of Jubilees* also supports the notion that while only a minority of spirits were allowed to remain active. "And the chief of the spirits, Mastêmâ, came and said: 'Lord, Creator, let some of them remain before me, and let them harken to my voice, and do all that I shall say unto them; for if some of them are not left to me, I shall not be able to execute the power of my will on the sons of men; for these are for corruption and leading astray before my judgment, for great is the wickedness of the sons of men.' And He said: Let the tenth part of them remain before him, and let nine parts descend into the place of condemnation.'" 10:8-9.

[18] See Kelley Coblentz Baruch, "What Becomes of the Angels' Wives? A Textual-Critical Study of 1 Enoch 19:2," *JBL* 125 (2006):766-80.

Enoch, alone saw the vision, the ends of all things: and no man shall see as I have seen."

In addition to the revelation concerning the angels that Enoch is given, all humans' future abode is also revealed to him. Enoch is informed of the following:

"1 And thence I went to another place, and he mountain [and] of hard rock. 2 And there was in it four hollow places, deep and wide and very smooth. How smooth are the hollow places and deep and dark to look at. 3 Then Raphael answered, one of the holy angels who was with me, and said unto me: 'These hollow places have been created for this very purpose, that the spirits of the souls of the dead should 4 assemble therein, yea that all the souls of the children of men should assemble here. And these places have been made to receive them till the day of their judgment and till their appointed period [till the period appointed], till the great judgment (comes) upon them.' I saw (the spirit of) a dead man making suit, 5 and his voice went forth to heaven and made suit. And I asked Raphael the angel who was 6 with me, and I said unto him: 'This spirit which maketh suit, whose is it, whose voice goeth forth and maketh suit to heaven' 7 And he answered me saying: 'This is the spirit which went forth from Abel, whom his brother Cain slew, and he makes his suit against him till his seed is destroyed from the face of the earth, and his seed is annihilated from amongst the seed of men.' 8 The I asked regarding it, and regarding all the hollow places: 'Why is one separated from the other' 9 And he answered me and said unto me: 'These three have been made that the spirits of the dead might be separated.'"

The spirits of the dead are divided among the righteous, among the wicked who have not had a judgment placed on their life, among those who were murdered unjustly, and lastly, another group of wicked who will not rise from this place on the day of judgment.[19] Enoch is then taken to see a mountain range where God's throne at the judgment is situated. Enoch sees a tree as well, the tree of life.

> "1 And he said unto me: 'Enoch, why dost thou ask me regarding the fragrance of the tree, 2 and why dost thou wish to learn the truth' Then I answered him saying: 'I wish to 3 know about everything, but especially about this tree.' And he answered saying: 'This high mountain which thou hast seen, whose summit is like the throne of God, is His throne, where the Holy Great One, the Lord of Glory, the Eternal King, will sit, when He shall come down to visit 4 the earth with goodness. And as for this fragrant tree, no mortal is permitted to touch it till the great judgment, when He shall take vengeance on all and bring (everything) to its consummation 5 forever. It shall then be

---

[19] I Enoch 22:8-9. James C. Vanderkam, *Enoch: A Man for All Generations* (Columbia: University of South Carolina, 1995), 54-55.

given to the righteous and holy. Its fruit shall be for food to the elect: it shall be transplanted to the holy place, to the temple of the Lord, the Eternal King.

6 Then shall they rejoice with joy and be glad, And into the holy place shall they enter; And its fragrance shall be in their bones, And they shall live a long life on earth, Such as thy fathers lived;"

The righteous are bound to return to a pristine earth, and a reversal of the fall of man will occur.[20] Another set of mountains and ravines are shown to Enoch. These reveal the place of condemnation for the wicked. I Enoch 27:1-5 relates the following details:

"1 Then said I: 'For what object is this blessed land, which is entirely filled with trees, and this 2 accursed valley between' Then Uriel, one of the holy angels who was with me, answered and said: 'This accursed valley is for those who are accursed for ever: Here shall all the accursed be gathered together who utter with their lips against the Lord unseemly words and of His glory speak hard things. Here shall they be gathered together, and here 3 shall be their place of judgment. In the last days there shall be upon them the spectacle of righteous judgment in the presence of the righteous forever: here shall the merciful bless the

---

[20] James C. Vanderkam, *Enoch: A Man for All Generations* (Columbia: University of South Carolina, 1995), 56.

Lord of glory, the Eternal King. 4 In the days of judgement over the former, they shall bless Him for the mercy in accordance with 5 which He has assigned them (their lot).' Then I blessed the Lord of Glory and set forth His glory and lauded Him gloriously."

His activity complements Enoch-Metatron's role as mediator and intercessor. In *Lamentations Rabbah*, Metatron intercedes on behalf of Israel when God decides to withdraw his Shekhinah from the Temple.

"At that time the Holy One, blessed be He, wept and said, 'Woe is Me! What have I done? I caused My Shechinah to dwell below on earth for the sake of Israel; but now that they have sinned, I have returned to My former habitation. Heaven forfend that I become a laughter to the nations and a byword to human beings!' At that time Metatron came, fell upon his face, and spake before the Holy One, blessed be He: 'Sovereign of the Universe, let me weep, but do Thou not weep.' He replied to him, 'If though lettest Me not weep now, I will repair to a place which though hast not permission to enter, and will weep there,' as it is said, But if ye will not hear it, My soul shall weep in secret for pride (Jeremiah 13:17)."[21]

---

[21] Midrash Rabbah 7.41. Andrei A. Orlov, *From Patriarch to the Youth: The Metatron Tradition in 2 Enoch,* PhD diss. (Milwaukee: Marquette University, 2004), 145.

Another example of Enoch-Metatron intervening on behalf of humanity is found in the example of Rabbi Ishmael, who ascends into heaven and is opposed by the angels. Enoch-Metatron defends him. 3 Enoch 2:1-4 states,

> "(1) In that hour, the eagles of the Merkaba, the flaming 'Ophanim and the Seraphim of consuming fire asked Metatron, saying to him:
>
> (2) 'Youth! Why sufferest thou one born of woman to enter and behold the Merkaba? From which nation, from which tribe is this one? What is his character?'
>
> (3) Metatron answered and said to them: 'From the nation of Israel whom the Holy One, blessed be He, chose for his people from among seventy tongues (nations), from the tribe of Levi, whom he set aside as a contribution to his name and from the seed of Aaron whom the Holy One, blessed be He, did choose for his servant and put upon him the crown of priesthood on Sinai.'
>
> (4) Forthwith, they spake and said: 'Indeed, this one is worthy to behold the Merkaba.' And they said: 'Happy is the people that is in such a case!'

Enoch as a Witness of God's Judgment

The shorter revised version of 2 Enoch relates Enoch's added role as an eschatological witness of God's judgment. Enoch is elevated to a new status.

"...and you will be in front of my face from now and forever. And you will be seeing my secrets, and you will be scribe for my servants...and you will be for me *a witness of the judgment* of the great age."[22]

The idea of Enoch as a witness or even participant in God's divine judgment may stem from Mesopotamian tradition. Members of the *baru* guild of diviners were sometimes assistants to Shamash and Adad. They were designated as the lords of decisions since they were responsible for judgment. One Mesopotamian text states:

"The *baru* shall seat himself before Shamash and Adad on the tribunal and the judge a judgment of right and righteousness. Shamash and Adad, the great gods, the Lords of vision, the Lords of decision, appear before him in order to decide a decision (and) answer him with a faithful yea."[23]

---

[22] F.I. Andersen, '2 (Slavonic Apocalypse of) Enoch', in J.H. Charlesworth, ed., *The Old Testament Pseudepigrapha Volume 1: Apocalyptic Literature and Testaments* (New York: Doubleday, 1983, 1985), 161. Andrei Orlov notes that in later Jewish mysticism, Enoch-Metatron is referred as the great angel (prince) of testimony. Andrei A. Orlov, *From Patriarch to the Youth: The Metatron Tradition in 2 Enoch,* PhD diss. (Milwaukee: Marquette University, 2004), 89.

[23] Alfred Ossian Haldar, *Associations of Cult Prophets Among the Ancient Semites* (Uppsala: Almqvist & Wiksells, 1945), 3.

CHAPTER 11

Enoch as a Messianic Figure

While the first part of I Enoch is concerned with the fallen angels and the punishments they deserve, the first book of Enoch does discuss events related to Israel's sacred history. The period of Israelite enslavement and the Exodus is discussed in I Enoch 89: 14-39. The giving of the Torah is mentioned twice. I Enoch 93:6 provides a reference to the giving of the Torah.

> "6 And after that in the fourth week, at its close,
> Visions of the holy and righteous shall be seen,
> And a law for all generations and an enclosure shall be made for them."

The extent of the angel's evil deeds is recounted in the ending chapters of I Enoch. I Enoch 106: 1-7 relates the birth of Noah and the supernormal nature of his birth. Lamech, Noah's father, is most concerned about his son's bizarre birth and radiance.

> "And after some days my son Methuselah took a wife for his son Lamech, and she became 2

pregnant by him and bore a son. And his body was white as snow and red as the blooming of a rose, and the hair of his head and his long locks were white as wool, and his eyes beautiful. And when he opened his eyes, he lighted up the whole house like the sun, and the whole house 3 was very bright. And thereupon he arose in the hands of the midwife, opened his mouth, and conversed with the Lord of righteousness. 4 And his father Lamech was afraid of him, and 5 fled, and came to his father, Methuselah. And he said unto him: ' I have begotten a strange son, diverse from and unlike man, and resembling the sons of the God of heaven; and his nature is different, and he is not like us, and his eyes are as the rays of the sun, and his 6 countenance is glorious. And it seems to me that he is not sprung from me but from the angels, and I fear that in his days a wonder may be 7 wrought on the earth."

The *Wisdom of Solomon* relates Enoch's ascent without specifically referencing him. Chapter 4:10-15 state:

> "[10] He pleased God, and was beloved of him: so that living among sinners he was translated.
> [11] Yea speedily was he taken away, lest that wickedness should alter his understanding, or deceit beguile his soul.
> [12] For the bewitching of naughtiness doth obscure things that are honest; and the wandering of concupiscence doth undermine the simple mind.

> [13] He, being made perfect in a short time, fulfilled a long time:
> [14] For his soul pleased the Lord: therefore hasted he to take him away from among the wicked.
> [15] This the people saw, and understood it not, neither laid they up this in their minds, That his grace and mercy is with his saints, and that he hath respect unto his chosen."

The term *Messiah* does not appear in I Enoch 1-36 and 91-104. The term appears twice in the section referred to as the *Similitudes of Enoch* or the *Book of Parables,* which consists of I Enoch 37-71. Enoch emphasizes the terms *Chosen* or *Elect One*.[1] He also highlights the *Son of Man*. The *Similitudes* also refer to this character as the *Righteous One* and the *Anointed One* or Messiah. I Enoch 48:10 states,

> "And on the day of their affliction there shall be rest on the earth, And before them, they shall fall and not rise again: And there shall be no one to take them with his hands and raise them: For they have denied the Lord of Spirits and *His Anointed*. The name of the Lord of Spirits be blessed."
> Chapter 52:3-4 states, "And I asked the angel who went with me, saying, 'What things are these which I have seen in (4) secret' and he said unto me: 'All these things which thou hast seen shall

---

[1] I Enoch 40:5;

serve the dominion of *His Anointed* that he may be potent and mighty on the earth.'"[2]

Andrei Orlov suggests that the four titles appear to be used interchangeably and denote one composite figure.[3] Most striking is the identification of Enoch with the *Son of Man*.

George Nickelsburg considers the possibility that the composite figure in the *Similitudes* of Enoch is drawn from various biblical images. The single image,

> "draws much of its language and imagery from three biblical sources or traditional interpretations of these sources. The basic texts: Daniel 7; Isaiah 11 and Psalm 2; Isaiah 42, 49, 52-53. Through the use and elaboration of this material, the author has created a composite figure whom he considers to be the referent in texts about the heavenly one like a son of man, the Davidic king, and Second Isaiah's servant of the Lord."[4]

I Enoch 70:17 also states:

---

[2] See also George W. E. Nickelsburg, "Salvation without and with a Messiah: Developing Beliefs in Writings Ascribed to Enoch," in the *Judaisms and their Messiahs at the Turn of the Christian Era*, ed. Jacob Neusner (Cambridge: Cambridge University, 1987), 49.

[3] Andrei A. Orlov, *From Patriarch to the Youth: The Metatron Tradition in 2 Enoch,* PhD diss. (Milwaukee: Marquette University, 2004), 109.

[4] George Nickelsburg, "Son of Man." in Anchor Bible Dictionary 6.138.

"Then that angel came to me, and with his voice saluted me, saying, You are the Son of man, who art born for righteousness, and righteousness has rested upon you."[5]

The importance of this passage and the entire section encompassing chapters 70-71. Commenting on this, Alan Segal states:

"This is an extraordinarily important event, as it underlines the importance of the mystic transformation between the adept and the angelic vice-regent of God."[6]

Andrei Orlov addresses the problem with Enoch's identification with the Son of Man figure since I Enoch 48:2-7 implies the latter is pre-existent. Orlov explains that this may be resolved by the view that a human being

---

[5] Translated from Ethiopic by Richard Laurence, *The Book of Enoch-The Prophet* (London: Kegan Paul, Trench & Co., 1883), 91. It is important to note that the original inclusion or placement of chapters 70-71 is often contested by scholars. Andrei Orlov states: "Some scholars believe that these chapters might represent later interpolation(s) and do not belong to the original text of the Book of the Similitudes. They note that these two chapters do not appropriately correspond with the tripartite structure of the Similitudes." Andrei A. Orlov, *From Patriarch to the Youth: The Metatron Tradition in 2 Enoch,* PhD diss. (Milwaukee: Marquette University, 2004), 110.

[6] A. Segal, "The Risen Christ and the Angelic Mediator Figures in Light of Qumran, " in *Jesus and the Dead Sea Scrolls*, ed. J. Charlesworth (New York: Doubleday, 1992), 305.

could have a heavenly twin or counterpart.⁷ Similar ideas can be found in multiple sources from the Second Temple period or the era following the Second Temple's destruction. The former includes the *Prayer of Joseph*. The post-Temple texts include sections from Targum Pseudo-Jonathan, Targum Neofiti, and the Fragmentary Targum.⁸ As one example, Targum Pseudo –Jonathan to Genesis 28:12 states:

> "He (Jacob) had a dream, and behold, a ladder was fixed in the earth with its top teaching toward the heavens…and on that day they (angels) ascended to the heavens on high, and said, 'Come and see Jacob the pious, whose image is fixed (engraved) in the Throne of Glory and whom you have desired to see."⁹

Perhaps most surprisingly, as the Enochic literature develops into Merkabah literature, i.e., *Sefer Hekhalot*, etc., the titles messiah, son of man, and righteous ones

---

⁷ Andrei A. Orlov, *From Patriarch to the Youth: The Metatron Tradition in 2 Enoch,* PhD diss. (Milwaukee: Marquette University, 2004), 111. See also James Vanderkam, "Righteous One, Messiah, Chosen One, and Son of Man in I Enoch 37-71), in *The Messiah: Developments in Earliest Judaism and Christianity. The First Princeton Symposium on Judaism and Christians Origins*, eds., J.H. Charlesworth et al (Minneapolis: Fortress, 1992), 182-183.

⁸ See also Genesis Rabbah 68:12; Number Rabbah 4:1; Bavli Hullin 91b; Pirque de Rabbi Eliezer 35. See also Matthew 18:10.

⁹ M. Maher, trans., *Targum Pseudo-Jonathan: Genesis: The Aramaic Bible 1B* (Collegeville: The Liturgical Press, 1992), 99-100.

almost entirely disappear.[10] Part of this may have been a Jewish reaction to the use or appropriation of these terms by the nascent Christian movement. The adoption of the term *Youth* for Enoch-Metatron may have served as a substitute for these terms.[11]

Enoch as the Son of Man

It is important to note that the *Astronomical Book*, the *Book of the Watchers*, the *Epistles of Enoch*, and the *Book of Dreams (Visions)* were all found in Cave 4 at Qumran. The *Similitudes of Enoch* appear to be missing. This may point to a later date for this section. The importance of the Similitudes of Enoch for the study of the New Testament is significant. The impact is, however, vigorously debated. As James Vanderkam states, the extent of its influence is disputed.

> "Some New Testament scholars have maintained that the use of this term [i.e., Son of Man] in the Gospels, especially Matthew, is indebted in some way to the Enochic usage of 'Son of Man' for a superhuman judge of the end time, while others, for various reasons, have held that the two- I

---

[10] Andrei A. Orlov, *From Patriarch to the Youth: The Metatron Tradition in 2 Enoch,* PhD diss. (Milwaukee: Marquette University, 2004), 113.

[11] Martin Hengel, *The Son of God: The Origin of Christology and the History of Jewish-Hellenistic Religion* (Eugene: Wipf & Stock Publishers, 2007), 46.

Enoch 37-71 and the Gospels- are independent of each other in their employment of the peculiar phrase. According to some scholars, the Similitudes were written later than the New Testament Gospels."[12]

The problem with the latter view that most scholars likely reject is the implications for early Christianity. James Vanderkam notes this when he states:

"It is extremely difficult to imagine that a Christian could have written this book, which credits Enoch with a major role assigned to Jesus in Christian eschatology."[13]

It is quite possible, I believe that a Christian may have modified the text to create an expectation of Jesus having been the true the fulfillment of this passage. The Messiah in Enoch does not refer to a king. It instead represents a transcendent, divine-like figure. However, as Nickelsburg points out, this term is usually qualified. That is, it occurs with a specific designation, such as "this Son of Man" or "that Son of Man" or "the Son of Man who..." Because of this, its designation as a title is questionable.[14]

The *Odes of Solomon* was likely written in Aramaic, though Hebrew and Greek have also been suggested.

---

[12] James C. Vanderkam, *Enoch: A Man for All Generations* (Columbia: University of South Carolina, 1995), 132.

[13] Ibid.,133.

[14] Ibid., 58. Rutherford H. Platt, ed., *The Forgotten Books of Eden* (New York: Alpha House, 1926).

The date of their composition is given anywhere from the 1st to the 3rd century. They may quite interestingly constitute, at least in part, a Jewish Christian hymn book. Ode 36 is quite similar to the *Book of Enoch* in representing the election of a human being to the status of God's son. This view reflected the views of some Jewish Christians. In 3 Enoch, Enoch acquires divine attributes.[15] Ode 36 states,

> "I rested in the Spirit of the Lord: and the Spirit raised me on high: 2 And made me stand on my feet in the height of the Lord, before His perfection and His glory, while I was praising Him by the composition of His songs. 3 The Spirit brought me forth before the face of the Lord: and, although a son of man, I was named the Illuminate, the Son of God: 4 While I praised amongst the praising ones, and great was I amongst the mighty ones. 5 For according to the greatness of the Most High, so He made me: and like His own newness He renewed me; and He anointed me from His own perfection: 6 And I became one of His Neighbors; and my mouth was opened; like a cloud of dew; 7 And my heart poured out as it were a gushing stream of righteousness, 8 And my access to Him was in peace; and I was established by the Spirit of His government. Hallelujah."

---

[15] Hugh Schonfield, *The History of Jewish Christianity* (London: Duckworth, 1936), 62, 64.

I Enoch's beginning chapters relate the intercession of angels who carry the plight of humanity to God. The angels implore their case. The story centers on the events of Genesis 9 and goes beyond this account, and points to an eschatological setting. The giants, the offspring of the forbidden sexual union of fallen angels and women, cause sweeping wickedness that exceeds human beings' evil practices. The *Damascus Document* found at Qumran relates the following:

> "Hear now, my sons, and I will uncover your eyes that you may see and understand the works of God, that you may choose that which pleases Him and reject that which He hates, that you may walk perfectly in all His ways and not follow afterthoughts of the guilty inclination and after eyes of lust. For through them, great men have gone astray, and mighty heroes have stumbled from former times till now. *Because they walked in the stubbornness of their heart, the Heavenly Watchers fell; they were caught because they did not keep the commandments of God. And their sons also fell who were tall as cedar trees and whose bodies were like mountains.* All flesh on dry land perished; they were as though they had never been because they did their own will and did not keep the commandment of their Maker so that His wrath was kindled against them. Through

it, the children of Noah went astray, together with their kin, and were cut off."[16]

The ultimate source of this evil is supernatural principalities and powers.

As a consequence, they can only be contested and defeated by divine intervention. I Enoch departs from the account in Genesis 6-9 and envisions angelic beings as *the* agents of judgment and redemption.[17] The angel Raphael, for example, fights Azazel. The latter is a fallen angel and one of the leaders of the Watchers. Azazel revealed magical spells to humanity but is himself bound by Raphael. The angel Gabriel engages the *gibborim* (the Mighty Ones) though he manages to have them fight each other. The angel, Michael, fights the giants and cleanses the earth. According to George Nickelsburg, the angels Raphael, Gabriel, and Michael function in ways parallel to human representatives. They perform the functions of a prophet; they heal, they are warriors and high priests. Each of these roles reflects a specific method of salvation.[18]

---

[16] Damascus Document 2:14-3:1. James C. Vanderkam, *Enoch: A Man for All Generations* (Columbia: University of South Carolina, 1995), 122.

[17] George W. E. Nickelsburg, "Salvation without and with a Messiah: Developing Beliefs in Writings Ascribed to Enoch," in *Judaisms and their Messiahs at the Turn of the Christian Era,* ed. Jacob Neusner (Cambridge: Cambridge University, 1987), 51.

[18] Ibid., 52.

In chapters 6-11, the angelic intercessors are replaced by Enoch. Whereas the angelic beings pleaded for humanity, Enoch implores on behalf of the condemned fallen angels, the *Fallen Watchers*. Enoch's appeal to God on behalf of the Watchers is unsuccessful. In chapter 14, he is both prophet and scribe. Enoch relates how God destined him to reveal heaven's admonishment.[19] Enoch describes that God will bring judgment to the Watchers. God's revelation is that of a great warrior.

The Wicked will be punished for their wicked deeds and blasphemous words. The righteous and chosen, however, will be forgiven and receive mercy and peace. The righteous will be the recipients of wisdom, which will keep them from sinning in either word or deed.[20] *I Enoch* 5:6 relates,

> "And there shall be forgiveness of sins,
> And every mercy and peace and forbearance:
> There shall be salvation unto them, a goodly light.
>
> And for all of you sinners, there shall be no salvation."[21]

The *Book of Parables* is unique in the Enochic corpus because of two elements. The first is its emphasis on salvation and judgment. The drama of the Divine throne

---

[19] Ibid., 53.
[20] Ibid., 53.
[21] R.H. Charles, *The Book of Enoch* (London: Society for Promotion of Christian Knowledge, 1917), 33-34.

room is described. The agent serves the judicial and salvific functions.[22] He is revealed to be in hiding.

> "(6a) And in that place mine eyes saw the Elect One of righteousness and of faith, (6b) *and I saw his dwelling-place under the wings of the Lord of Spirits.* (7a) and righteousness shall prevail in his days, and the righteous and elect shall be without number before Him forever and ever. (7b) and all the righteous and elect before Him shall be strong as fiery lights, and their mouth shall be full of blessing…"[23]

The Chosen and Anointed One

God prepares for judgment. The agent of judgment is the *Elect* or *Chosen one*. 45:3-4 states:

> "3 On that day Mine Elect One shall sit on the throne of glory and shall try their works, And their places of rest shall be innumerable.
>
> And their souls shall grow strong within them when they see Mine Elect Ones, and those who have called upon My glorious name: 4 Then will I cause Mine Elect One to dwell among them."[24]

---

[22] George W. E. Nickelsburg, "Salvation without and with a Messiah: Developing Beliefs in Writings Ascribed to Enoch," in *Judaisms and their Messiahs at the Turn of the Christian Era,* ed. Jacob Neusner (Cambridge: Cambridge University, 1987), 56.

[23] I Enoch 39:6-7.

[24] See also I Enoch 55:4; 69:29.

An explicit reference to *a* Messiah occurs in chapters 37-71, the *Book of Parables*. As noted, the Messiah of Enoch is not a Davidic King or a Levitical priest. He is a divine-like heavenly figure with names and roles taken from several biblical eschatological settings.[25] I Enoch 46:1-6 states:

> "1 And there I saw One who had a head of days, And His head was white like wool, *And with Him was another being whose countenance had the appearance of a man, And his face was full of graciousness, like one of the holy angels.* 2 And I asked the angel who went with me and showed me all the hidden things, concerning that 3 Son of Man, who he was, and whence he was, (and) why he went with the Head of Days and he answered and said unto me: *This is the son of Man who hath righteousness, With whom dwelleth righteousness, and who revealeth all the treasures of that which is hidden,* because the Lord of Spirits hath chosen him, and whose lot hath the pre-eminence before the Lord of Spirits in uprightness forever.
>
> 4 *And this Son of Man whom thou hast seen Shall raise up the kings, and the mighty from their seats, [And the strong from their thrones] ad*

---

[25] George W. E. Nickelsburg, "Salvation without and with a Messiah: Developing Beliefs in Writings Ascribed to Enoch," in *Judaisms and their Messiahs at the Turn of the Christian Era*, ed. Jacob Neusner (Cambridge: Cambridge University, 1987), 56.

shall loosen the reins of the strong, And break the teeth of the sinners.

5 [And he shall put down the kings from their thrones and kingdoms] Because they do not extol and praise Him, nor humbly acknowledge whence the kingdom was bestowed upon them. 6 And he shall put down the countenance of the strong, And shall fill them with shame."[26]

The angels, who previously exercised punishment on Azazel and his fellow angels who have lead man astray and the wicked kings who have oppressed the righteous, are much less prominent now than in Chapters 6-11. The principal-agent of judgment this time is the chief representative of the heavenly court. His face gleams like an angel. He surpasses all other beings in the heavenly court. Also, the righteous who have been persecuted participate in the judgment of the Wicked through the agency of the Chosen One.[27]

In the Book of Parables, the messianic figure also executes divine judgment against the fallen angels, the wicked kings, and the mighty ones. The Son of Man judges and *is even placed on God's magnificent throne.*

---

[26] See also I Enoch 48:1-7.

[27] I Enoch 48: 2-7. George W. E. Nickelsburg, "Salvation without and with a Messiah: Developing Beliefs in Writings Ascribed to Enoch," in *Judaisms and their Messiahs at the Turn of the Christian Era,* ed. Jacob Neusner (Cambridge: Cambridge University, 1987), 63.

"And one portion of them shall look on the other, and they shall be terrified, and they shall be downcast of countenance, and pain shall seize them when they see *that Son of Man* sitting on the throne of his glory.

6 And the kings and the mighty and all who possess the earth shall bless and glorify and extol him who rules over all, who was hidden.

7 For from the beginning, *the Son of Man was hidden*, and the Most High preserved him in the presence of His might and revealed him to the elect.

8 And the congregation of the elect and holy shall be sown, and all the elect shall stand before him on that day.

9 And all the kings and the mighty and the exalted and those who rule the earth shall fall down before him on their faces, and worship and set their hope upon *that Son of Man*, and petition him and supplicate for mercy at his hands."[28]

The passage introduces a figure that has a human-like face but is glorious like an angel. This figure is the highest representative of the heavenly court. He surpasses the angels Michael, Raphael, Gabriel, and Phanuel. His

---

[28] I Enoch 62:4-9. See R.H. Charles, *The Book of Enoch* (London; Society for Promotion of Christian Knowledge, 1917).

righteousness will be reflected in his judgment.[29] The Messiah is ascribed great righteousness as the bearer of divine secrets, and even victory over the strong and the wicked.[30] In this role, the Son of Man was held to be a bearer of redemption and judgment at the end of days.

In I Enoch 47, which appears related to Daniel 7, the Head of Days is seated on his throne in the middle of the angelic court. The books of the living are opened. The righteous that have died are to be avenged.[31] The text, however, turns to the appointing of the Son of Man. I Enoch 48:2-7 relates,

---

[29] George W. E. Nickelsburg, "Salvation without and with a Messiah: Developing Beliefs in Writings Ascribed to Enoch," in *Judaisms and their Messiahs at the Turn of the Christian Era,* ed. Jacob Neusner (Cambridge: Cambridge University, 1987), 59. I Enoch 62:3 states: "And there shall stand up in that day all the kings and the mighty, And the exalted and those who hold the earth, And they shall see and recognize How he sits on the throne of his glory, And righteousness is judged before him, And no lying word is spoken before him."

[30] I Enoch 37-71.

[31] I Enoch 47:1-2 "And in those days shall have ascended the prayer of the righteous, and the blood of the righteous from the earth before the Lord of Spirits. In those days the holy ones who dwell above in the heavens Shall unite with one voice And supplicate and pray [and praise, And give thanks and bless the name of the Lord of Spirits] On behalf of the blood of the righteous which has been shed, And that the prayer of the righteous may not be in vain before the Lord of Spirits, That judgment may be done unto them, And that they may not have to suffer forever." See also I Enoch 47:4.

"And in that place, I saw the fountain of righteousness Which was inexhaustible: And around it were many fountains of wisdom: And all the thirsty drank of them, And were filled with wisdom, And their dwellings were with the righteous and holy and elect. 2 And at that hour that Son of Man was named In the presence of the Lord of Spirits, and his name before the Head of Days.

3 Yea, before the sun and the signs were created, before the stars of the heaven were made, His name was named before the Lord of Spirits.

4 He shall be a staff to the righteous whereon to stay themselves and not fall, and he shall be the light of the Gentiles, and the hope of those who are troubled of heart.

5 All who dwell on earth shall fall down and worship before him and will praise and bless and celebrate with song the Lord of Spirits.

6 And for this reason, hath he been chosen and hidden before Him, before the creation of the world and forevermore.

7 And the wisdom of the Lord of Spirits hath revealed him to the holy and righteous; For he hath preserved the lot of the righteous, Because they have hated and despised this world of unrighteousness, And have hated all its works and ways in the name of the Lord of Spirits: For in his

name they are saved, And according to his good pleasure hath it been in regard to their life."[32]

I Enoch 48:3 indicates that the Son of Man was in God's mind before creation. He has been revealed to the holy ones only more recently.[33] Features present in Daniel 7:13-14 and the *Servant* figure in Isaiah 40-55 were attributed to him as well.[34] Furthermore, the link between this figure and God's ultimate plan for humanity were interrelated. I Enoch 49:1-4 relates,

> "1 For wisdom is poured out like water, And glory faileth not before him for evermore.
>
> 2 For he is mighty in all the secrets of righteousness, and unrighteousness shall disappear as a shadow, and have no continuance; Because the Elect One standeth before the Lord of Spirits, and his glory is forever and ever, and his might unto all generations.
>
> 3 And in him dwells the spirit of wisdom, and the spirit which gives insight, and the spirit of understanding and of might, and the spirit of those who have fallen asleep in righteousness.
>
> 4 And he shall judge the secret things, and none shall be able to utter a lying word before

---

[32] I Enoch 48: 2-7. R.H. Charles, *The Book of Enoch* (London; Society for Promotion of Christian Knowledge, 1917), 66-67. See Isaiah 11, 42, 49, and Psalm 2.

[33] James C. Vanderkam, *Enoch: A Man for All Generations*, (Columbia: University of South Carolina, 1995), 139.

[34] Larry W. Hurtado, *One God, One Lord* (Minneapolis: Fortress Press, 1988), 54.

him; For he is the Elect One before the Lord of Spirits according to His good pleasure."[35]

The *Elect One* can judge because he is in the presence of the Lord of Spirits. The connection, according to George Nickelsburg, is drawn from Isaiah 42:1.[36] The prophet Isaiah states:

"Behold my servant, whom I uphold, my Chosen One in whom my soul delights; I have put my spirit upon him, he will bring forth justice to the nations."

The story in I Enoch continues with an expectation of impending judgment. The wicked kings of the earth are flung down. The kings are to be judged because they denied the Lord of Spirits and his Anointed One.[37] Enoch

---

[35] I Enoch 49:1-4. R.H. Charles, *The Book of Enoch* (London; Society for Promotion of Christian Knowledge, 1917), 67-68.

[36] George W. E. Nickelsburg, "Salvation without and with a Messiah: Developing Beliefs in Writings Ascribed to Enoch," in *Judaisms and their Messiahs at the Turn of the Christian Era,* ed. Jacob Neusner (Cambridge: Cambridge University, 1987), 61. Interestingly, the Septuagint translation of Isaiah 42:1 identifies the servant specifically as Jacob. "Jacob is my servant; I will lay hold of him; Israel is my chosen; my soul has accepted him; I have put my spirit upon him." Moises Silva, trans. *Esaias: A New English Translation of the Septuagint* (New York: Oxford University Press, 2009), 856.

[37] I Enoch 48:10, "And on the day of their affliction there shall be rest on the earth, and before them they shall fall and not rise again: And there shall be no one to take them with his hands and raise them: For they have denied the Lord of Spirits and His

is shown the pending judgment of those who are rebellious against God. He is also shown that the Righteous and Elect one will appear.

> "1 There mine eyes saw a deep valley with open mouths, and all who dwell on the earth and sea and islands shall bring to him gifts and presents and tokens of homage, but that deep valley shall not become full. 2 And their hands commit lawless deeds, And the sinners devour all whom they lawlessly oppress: Yet the sinners shall be destroyed before the face of the Lord of Spirits, And they shall be banished from off the face of His earth, And they shall perish for ever and ever. 3 For I saw all the angels of punishment abiding (there) and preparing all the instruments of Satan. 4 And I asked the angel of peace who went with me: 'For whom are they preparing these Instruments' 5 And he said unto me: 'They prepare these for the kings and the mighty of this earth, that they may thereby be destroyed. *6 And after this the Righteous and Elect One shall cause the house of his congregation to appear*: henceforth they shall be no more hindered in the name of the Lord of Spirits. 7 And these mountains shall not stand as the earth before his righteousness, But the hills shall be as a fountain

---

Anointed. The name of the Lord of Spirits be blessed." R.H. Charles, *The Book of Enoch* (London; Society for Promotion of Christian Knowledge, 1917), 66.

of water, And the righteous shall have rest from the oppression of sinners.'"[38]

The description of pending judgment reaches its culmination in Chapters 61-63. The scene is the heavenly court full of the angelic hosts. God seats the *Elect One* on His throne. Chapter 61:8-9 states,

"And the Lord of Spirits placed the Elect one on the throne of glory.

And he shall judge all the works of the holy above in the heaven, And in the balance shall their deeds be weighed

And when he shall lift up his countenance

To judge their secret ways according to the word of the name of the Lord of Spirits, And their path according to the way of the righteous judgment of the Lord of Spirits,

Then shall they all with one voice speak and bless, And glorify and extol and sanctify the name of the Lord of Spirits."[39]

---

[38] I Enoch 53:1-7.

[39] I Enoch 61:8-9. R.H. Charles, *The Book of Enoch* (London; Society for Promotion of Christian Knowledge, 1917), 89. See also I Enoch 51:1-3 which states: "1 And in those days shall the earth also give back that which has been entrusted to it, And Sheol also shall give back that which it has received, And hell shall give back that which it owes. 5a For in those days the Elect One shall arise, 2 And he shall choose the righteous and holy from among them: For the day has drawn nigh that they should be saved.3 And

Larry Hurtado comments that the chosen one appears to,

> "To act as judge on God's behalf ('in the name of the Lord of Spirits,' e.g., I Enoch 55:4) and in this capacity sits upon a throne that is closely linked with God: 'On that day the Chose One will sit on the throne of Glory' (45:3; see also 51:3; 55:4; 61:18; 62:2,3,5-6:70:27). The meaning of this is not that the figure rivals God or becomes a second god but rather that he is seen as performing the eschatological functions associated with God and is, therefore, God's chief agent, linked with God's work to a specially intense degree."[40]

The emerging figure retains elements of the archetypes but also incorporates some differences. The Son of Man corresponds to the figure of Daniel 9. I Enoch, however, he appears in the heavenly court to enact justice. In the book of Daniel, the Son of Man appears *after* the judgment.[41] In I Enoch, the wicked are judged by the

---

the Elect One shall in those days sit on My throne, And his mouth shall pour forth all the secrets of wisdom and counsel: For the Lord of Spirits hath given (them) to him and hath glorified him."

[40] Larry Hurtado, *One God, One Lord* (Minneapolis: Fortress Press, 1988), 53.

[41] The *Wisdom of Solomon* includes a Servant figure who has been persecuted by wicked men. He judges them. The *Wisdom of Solomon* 5:1-5 states: "[1] Then the righteous man will stand with great confidence in the presence of those who have afflicted him, and those who make light of his labors. [2] When they see him, they will be shaken with dreadful fear, and they will be amazed at his unexpected salvation. [3] They will speak to one another in repentance, and in anguish of spirit they will groan, and say, [4]

Chosen One, who defends the cause of the chosen ones whom the wicked have oppressed.[42] Finally, the Anointed One, who executes God's justice on earthly rulers, is not a human king descended from David, but a member of the heavenly entourage. This last point is especially noteworthy since other documents, though not all, envisioned a future Davidic king of the Second Temple era.[43]

The *Wisdom of Solomon*, likely written around the first century CE, viewed Enoch as *the* example of righteousness.

> "There was one who pleased God and was loved by him, and while living among sinners, he was taken up. He was caught up lest evil change his understanding or guile deceive his soul. For the fascination of wickedness obscures what is good,

---

"This is the man whom we once held in derision and made a byword of reproach -- we fools! We thought that his life was madness and that his end was without honor. [5] Why has he been numbered among the sons of God? And why is his lot among the saints?" See also George W. E. Nickelsburg, "Salvation without and with a Messiah: Developing Beliefs in Writings Ascribed to Enoch," in *Judaisms and their Messiahs at the Turn of the Christian Era,* ed. Jacob Neusner (Cambridge: Cambridge University, 1987), 63.

[42] I Enoch 62-63.

[43] Nickelsburg's interpretation is of a future son of David that will fight against the Romans. George W. E. Nickelsburg, "Salvation without and with a Messiah: Developing Beliefs in Writings Ascribed to Enoch," in *Judaisms and their Messiahs at the Turn of the Christian Era,* ed. Jacob Neusner (Cambridge: Cambridge University, 1987), 63.

and roving desire perverts the innocent mind. Being perfected in a short time, he fulfilled long years; for his soul was pleasing to the Lord. Therefore he took him quickly from the midst of wickedness. Yet the peoples saw and did not understand, nor take such a thing to heart, that God's grace and mercy are with his elect, and he watches over his holy ones."[44]

George W.E. Nickelsburg summarizes the impact of I Enoch's imagery on the early Christian message.

"...the form of the Parables that identifies the exalted figure with Enoch and the closely related tradition in the Wisdom of Solomon testify to a situation in Judaism that may well have facilitated the claim of primitive Christianity *that a particular persecuted righteous one had been exalted as the unique Chosen One, Son of Man, and Messiah.*" [45]

---

[44] Wisdom of Solomon 4:10-15. See also Psalm 2 for a comparison between the righteous and his persecutors.

[45] George W. E. Nickelsburg, "Salvation without and with a Messiah: Developing Beliefs in Writings Ascribed to Enoch," in *Judaisms and their Messiahs at the Turn of the Christian Era,* ed. Jacob Neusner (Cambridge: Cambridge University, 1987), 64.

CHAPTER 12

Enoch and the Angels

The angels, i.e., the Fallen Watchers, have been partly discussed in previous chapters. The texts ascribed to I Enoch, widely accepted to date from the third-century B.C.E, embrace the view that Enoch's relationship with God was mediated through angels. The *Book of Enoch* begins,

> "The words of blessing of Enoch according to which he blessed the chosen and righteous who must be present on the day of distress (which is appointed) for the removal of all the wicked and impious. And Enoch answered and said there was) a righteous man whose eyes were opened by the Lord, and he saw a holy vision in the heavens which the angels showed to me. And I heard everything from them, and I understood what I saw, but not for this generation, but for a distant generation which will come." (1:1-3a).[1]

---

[1] This passage should be viewed in light of Genesis 5:22 "…he walked with the *elohim*."

James Vanderkam highlights that Enoch's words are similar to those of Moses in Deuteronomy 33 when the latter gives his farewell address to Israel's nation. More striking is the similarity that exists with Numbers 22-24. These chapters relate the episode of Balaam, the diviner. Balaam is hired by the Midianite and the Moabites to curse Israel. The similarities between Enoch's address and Balaam lie in the following: 1) Balaam is described as taking up his parable (Numbers 23-24 uses this term seven times); 2) Balaam's eyes were opened (Numbers 22:31, 23:3-4, 15-16); 3) Balaam saw a vision of God (Numbers 24:4, 15); 4) Balaam speaks of the distant future (Numbers 24:14, 17).[2]

The text of Genesis 6:1-2 relates the critical passage associated with the fallen angels.

> "And it came to pass when men began to multiply on the face of the earth, and daughters were born unto them, 2 that the sons of God saw the daughters of men that they were fair; and they took them wives, whomsoever they chose."

While the prevailing rabbinic view on the passage has been to reject any notion that *benei ha-elohim*, are divine beings, the literature bearing the Enoch's name embraced a very different view. It is important to note that there were exceptions. The idea that the *benei elohim* were in angels is not entirely unfounded in rabbinic thought. The Torah commentary Yalkut Me'am Loez

---

[2] James C. VanderKam, *Enoch: A Man for All Generations* (Columbia: University of South Carolina, 1995), 26-27.

Devarim 5, for example, states that two angels, Shamchazai and Uziel, descended to the world and married women from whom giants, as well as demons, were born.³

The *Book of Watchers* (I Enoch 1-36) elucidates the Genesis passage to conclude that the *Sons of God* were angels who had descended and taken women as their wives. I Enoch 6:1-2 states:

> "And it was when the sons of mankind became numerous, in those days beautiful and lovely daughters were born to them, and the angels, the sons of heaven, saw them and desired them, and they said among themselves, 'Come on, let's choose for ourselves wives from the sons of mankind and let's have sons for ourselves.'"

---

³ "What will happen to the world?" asked God. "We will be in the world," replied the angels. "But if you will be in the world," said God, "the evil urge will have power over you and you will sin even more than human beings who were created from the dust. If Adam sinned with one woman you will sin with many women." The two angels said, "Give us permission and we will be sent to the earth. We will show how we will sanctify Your name in the world." "Go down and live with the humans." When the two angels were sent to earth, the evil urge affected them and they did wrong. They began to fornicate with the most beautiful women in the world and could not hold back their desire…they sired great giants who were so tall that they covered the sun. One of them was Og, the king of the Bashan. He gave rise to a great family were sextuplets were often born." Rabbi Yitzchok Behar Arguiti, *The Torah Anthology Me'am Loez* (New York: Maznaim Publishing, 1984), 220-222.

According to I Enoch 6:6, the angels, i.e., the Fallen Watchers, descended to earth during the days of Enoch's father, Jared, which may be a play on the word *yarad* [4] meaning to come or go down or descend. Genesis states in 6:4,

הַנְּפִלִים הָיוּ בָאָרֶץ, בַּיָּמִים הָהֵם, וְגַם אַחֲרֵי-כֵן אֲשֶׁר יָבֹאוּ בְּנֵי הָאֱלֹהִים אֶל-בְּנוֹת הָאָדָם, וְיָלְדוּ לָהֶם: הֵמָּה הַגִּבֹּרִים אֲשֶׁר מֵעוֹלָם, אַנְשֵׁי הַשֵּׁם.

> "the *Nephilim*[5] were in the earth in those days, and also after that when the sons of God came in unto the daughters of men, and they bore children to them; the same were the mighty men that were of old, the men of renown."

The most common rendering of the word *Nephilim* is giants as corroborated by the Greek translation of Genesis 6, which renders *Nephilim* and *Gibborim* as giants.[6]

---

[6] The *Wisdom of Sirach* or *Ecclesiasticus* 16:7 states, "He [God] did not forgive the ancient giants who revolted in their might." Interestingly, the Hebrew text substitutes princes of old, for ancient giants. James C. VanderKam, *Enoch: A Man for All Generations* (Columbia: University of South Carolina, 1995), 107. Regarding Greek translations of the Bible, Chris Seeman notes, "The second century CE saw a proliferation of alternative Greek translations of the Bible, the most famous of which-those of Theodotion, Aquila, and Symmachus, were preserved in Origen's Hexapla. These translations share a tendency to 'correct' LXX in accordance with the emerging standardized Hebrew text. In the case of our passage, however, only Theodotion stands in continuity with what would later become the MT reading. Aquila renders… 'sons of the god'… probably meaning 'worshippers of the gods, idolaters.' Symmachus departs even more radically

However, the word's root may serve to indicate a connection to the idea of angels having descended or fallen from the original state.⁷ According to Enoch, the angel named Shemihazah secured two hundred angels' assurances in his plan to descend to earth and marry women.

> "'I fear ye will not 4 indeed agree to do this deed, and I alone shall have to pay the penalty of a great sin.' And they all answered him and said: 'Let us all swear an oath, and all bind ourselves by mutual imprecations 5 not to abandon this plan but to do this thing.' Then sware they all together and bound themselves 6 by mutual imprecations upon it. And they were in all two hundred; who descended in the days of Jared on the summit of Mount Hermon, and they called it Mount Hermon, because they had sworn 7 and bound themselves by mutual imprecations upon it. And these are the names of their leaders: Samlazaz, their leader, Araklba, Rameel, Kokablel, Tamlel, Ramlel, Danel, Ezeqeel, Baraqijal, 8 Asael, Armaros, Batarel, Ananel, Zaq1el, Samsapeel,

---

from the Hebrew with 'sons of the powerful ones', a development with parallels in early rabbinic literature." Chris Seeman, "The Watchers Traditions and Gen 6:1-4 (MT and LXX)," in Angela Kim Harkins, Kelley Coblentz Bautch, and John C. Endres, eds., *The Watchers in Jewish and Christian Traditions* (Minneapolis: Fortress Press, 2014), 35.

⁷ Fall, lie from Richard Whitaker, *Revised Brown-Driver-Briggs Hebrew-English Lexicon*, 1995.

Satarel, Turel, Jomjael, Sariel. These are their chiefs of tens."

The rebellious angels proceeded with their plan. After taking women as wives, they further violate the division between the divine and humans by revealing hidden knowledge to their spouses.

> "1 And all the others together with them took unto themselves wives, and each chose for himself one, and they began to go in unto them and to defile themselves with them, and they taught them charms 2 and enchantments, and the cutting of roots, and made them acquainted with plants."

I Enoch 8:1-3 provides greater detail on the specific knowledge each fallen angel revealed.

> "1 And Azazel taught men to make swords, and knives, and shields, and breastplates, and made known to them the metals of the earth and the art of working them, and bracelets, and ornaments, and the use of antimony, and the beautifying of the eyelids, and all kinds of costly stones, and all 2 colouring tinctures. And there arose much godlessness, and they committed fornication, and they 3 were led astray and became corrupt in all their ways. Semjaza taught enchantments and root-cuttings, 'Armaros the resolving of enchantments, Baraqijal (taught) astrology, Kokabel the constellations, Ezeqeel the knowledge of the clouds, Araqiel the signs of the earth, Shamsiel the signs of the sun, and Sariel the course of the

moon. And as men perished, they cried, and their cry went up to heaven . . ."

George Nicklesburg points to a Greek version of Enoch preserved by Syncellus. Nicklesburg used this translation to reconstruct an Aramaic fragment of 1 Enoch. 8:1-2. This reconstruction reads,

> "Asael taught men to make swords and weapons and shields and breastplates. And he showed them the metals of the earth and fold and the working of them. And they made them into bracelets and ornaments for women, and he showed them silver and stibium and eyepaint and select stones and dyes. And the sons of men made them for themselves and their daughters, and they transgressed and lead the holy ones astray. And there was much godlessness on the earth. And they committed fornication and went astray and made all their paths desolate."[8]

Interestingly, in the Greek work, *Prometheus Bound*, divination, pharmacology, and metallurgy are seen as interrelated. The Greek historian Diodorus Siculus pointed to Ephorus of Cyme who cited the *Dactyls*, a mythical race of men, as the "sorcerers, who practiced charms and initiatory rites and mysteries." They also taught mankind about the "use of fire and what the

---

[8] George W. E. Nickelsburg, "Apocalyptic and Myth in 1 Enoch 6-11,"Journal of Biblical Literature Vol. 96, No. 3 (1977):397.

metals copper and iron are, as well as the means of working them." (5.64,4-5).[9]

As far as the author of I Enoch is concerned, the knowledge the angels revealed to their wives and the rest of humanity is forbidden knowledge. They may reflect knowledge angels are expected to comprehend. In the hands of humans, however, such knowledge only serves a negative role.

I Enoch continues in 7:1 by relating the consequences of the union between angels and humans.[10]

> "And they 3 became pregnant, and they bare great giants, whose height was three thousand ells [cubits]: Who consumed 4 all the acquisitions of men. And when men could no longer sustain them, the giants turned against 5 them and devoured mankind. And they began to sin against birds, and beasts, and reptiles, and 6 fish, and to devour one another's flesh, and drink the blood. Then the earth laid accusation against the lawless ones."

---

[9] Annette Yoshiko Reed, *Fallen Angels and the History of Judaism and Christianity: The Reception of Enochic Literature* (Cambridge: Cambridge University Press, 2005), 40.

[10] Ida Frohlich notes that "The Book of Giants qualifies their relation as a case of *zenut* [i.e. sexual immorality] (4Q203 8, 9), one of the main categories of ethical impurities." Ida Frohlich, "Mesoptamian Elements and the Watchers Traditions," in Angela Kim Harkins, Kelley Coblentz Bautch, and John C. Endres, eds., *The Watchers in Jewish and Christian Traditions* (Minneapolis: Fortress Press, 2014), 15.

Regarding the Greek figure Prometheus, Anathea Portier-Young explains,

"Prometheus played an important role in the Greek myth of Titanomachy, or the war between the Olympian gods and the Titans (a generation of gods older than the Olympians) that would give the Olympians rule in heaven and confine the Titans to Tartaros. Closely, related to the Titanomachy, was the myth of gigantomachy in which the earth (Gaia) angered by the imprisonment of the defeated Titans, roused her children the Giant to challenge the rule established by the Olympians through their earlier victory. By the fifth century BCE, the two myths frequently merged, paving the way for the creative adaptation of elements from both traditions in the Book of the Watchers."[11]

---

[11] Anathea Portier-Young, " Symbolic Resistance in the *Book of the Watchers*," in Angela Kim Harkins, Kelley Coblentz Bautch, and John C. Endres, eds., *The Watchers in Jewish and Christian Traditions* (Minneapolis: Fortress Press, 2014), 43-44.

The Giants[12] wreaked havoc throughout the land.[13] They resorted to cannibalism and even consumed blood. The Giants committed transgressions that violated the most elementary human laws later designated as the Noachide laws.[14] Ida Frohlich compares the Giants to Mesopotamian demons.

> "The characteristics of the Giants evoke the Mesopotamian tradition about the *utukku-s,* a term generally used for demonic beings. The Enochic Giants have the same characteristics as the Mesopotamian demons; they are tall and obtrusive beings, roaming in bands, attacking their victims indiscriminately. They ravage the work of humans, devour the flesh of animals and humans, and consume their blood. They are born from a

---

[12] 4Q180-4Q181 in the Dead Sea Scrolls concur with the interpretation of the I Enoch. The Scrolls note, "7[And] Pesher concerning Azaz'el and the Angels 'wh[o went into the daughters of men] 8 [and] they [gave] birth to giants for them.' And concerning Azaz'el [who led them astray to deceit] 9 [to love] iniquity and to case to inherit wickedness, all their Pe[riod for destruction] 10 [with jealou]sy of judgments and the judgments of the council." James C. VanderKam, *Enoch: A Man for All Generations* (Columbia: University of South Carolina, 1995), 123.

[13] David Suter compares the violence depicted in the Book of Enoch to the wars undertaken by Alexander the Great's successors, the Diadochi. David Suter, "Fallen Angel, Fallen Priest: The Problem of Family Purity in 1 Enoch 6—16," Hebrew Union College Annual Vol. 50 (1979):115-135. See also George W. E. Nickelsburg, "Apocalyptic and Myth in 1 Enoch 6-11,"Journal of Biblical Literature Vol. 96, No. 3 (1977):383-405.

[14] James C. VanderKam, *Enoch: A Man for All Generations* (Columbia: University of South Carolina, 1995), 35.

sexual union of heavenly and earthly beings, considered in the Enochic story to be impure."¹⁵

Genesis 6:11 relates that as a consequence of the Giant's actions,

וַתִּשָּׁחֵת הָאָרֶץ, לִפְנֵי הָאֱלֹהִים; וַתִּמָּלֵא הָאָרֶץ, חָמָס.

"And the earth was corrupt before God, and the earth was filled with violence."

James Vanderkam suggests, however, that the phrase *lifnei ha-elohim* would have been rendered by the author of Enoch as follows:

"the earth was corrupt before *the angels*, and the earth was filled with violence."¹⁶

This translation is consistent with the rendering *ha-elohim* as angels in I Enoch. The dire state of affairs draws

---

¹⁵ Ida Frohlich, "Mesoptamian Elements and the Watchers Traditions," in Angela Kim Harkins, Kelley Coblentz Bautch, and John C. Endres, eds., *The Watchers in Jewish and Christian Traditions* (Minneapolis: Fortress Press, 2014), 17.

¹⁶ Ida Frohlich observes that "The purity system of ancient Israel is acquainted not only with physical impurities, but also ethical ones. Ethical impurity grows out of situations that are controllable and are not natural or necessary, such as delaying purification from physical impurity, polluting specific *sancta*, sexual transgressions, idolatry, and murder. Ida Frohlich, "Mesoptamian Elements and the Watchers Traditions," in Angela Kim Harkins, Kelley Coblentz Bautch, and John C. Endres, eds., *The Watchers in Jewish and Christian Traditions* (Minneapolis: Fortress Press, 2014), 15.

the attention of the four special angels which serve God. I Enoch 9:1-4 states:

> "1 And then Michael, Uriel, Raphael, and Gabriel looked down from heaven and saw much blood being 2 shed upon the earth, and all lawlessness being wrought upon the earth. And they said one to another: 'The earth made without inhabitant cries the voice of their crying up to the gates of heaven.' 3 And now to you, the holy ones of heaven, the souls of men make their suit, saying, 'Bring our cause 4 before the Most High.'"

In I Enoch, Enoch plays a role of intermediary between the fallen angels and those angels which remained loyal to the service of God:

> "...the Watchers [the good ones] called to me, Enoch the scribe, and said to me: 'Enoch, scribe of righteousness, go, inform the Watchers of heaven who have left the high heaven and the holy eternal place, and have corrupted themselves with the women, and have done as the sons of men do, and have taken wives for themselves, and have become completely corrupt on the earth. They will have on earth neither peace nor forgiveness of sin... (12:3-5)'" [17]

---

[17] R. H. Charles, *The Book of Enoch* (Oxford: Clarendon Press, 1912). The Testament of Abraham relates a tour of the world given to Abraham by the angel Michael just before his passing. Michael transports Abraham to the place of judgment and relates the following: "'And the one who produces (the evidence) is the

Enoch serves as a messenger and relays this message to the fallen angels, who, in turn, request his assistance.

> "Then I went and spoke to them all together, and they were all afraid; fear and trembling seized them. And they asked me to write out for them the record of a petition that they might receive forgiveness, and to take the record of their petition up to the Lord in heaven. For they (themselves) were not able from then on to speak, and they did not raise their eyes to heaven out of shame for their sins for which they had been condemned. And then I wrote out the record of their petition and their supplication in regard to their spirits and the deeds of each of them, and in regard to what they

---

teacher of heaven and earth and the scribe of righteousness, Enoch. For the Lord sent them here in order that they might record the sins and righteous deeds of each person.' And Abraham said, 'How can Enoch bear the weight of the souls, since he has not seen death? Or how can he give the sentence of all the souls?' And Michael said, 'If he were to give sentence concerning them, it would not be accepted, But it is not Enoch's business to give sentence; rather, the Lord is the one who gives sentence, and it is this one's (Enoch's) task only to write. For Enoch prayed to the Lord saying, 'Lord, I do not want to give the sentence of the souls, lest I become oppressive to someone.' And the Lord said to Enoch, 'I shall command you to write the sins of a soul that makes atonement, and it will enter into life. And if the souls has not made atonement and repented, you will find its sins (already) written, and it will be cast into punishment.'(11:3-10). James C. Vanderkam, Enoch: *A Man for All Generations* (Columbia: University of South Carolina, 1995), 156-157.

asked (namely) that they should obtain absolution and forbearance."[18]

The Watchers

The first reference to *Watchers* is found in Daniel 4. The first occurrence is Daniel 4: 10. The Babylonian King Nebuchadnezzar states:

> "I saw in the visions of my head upon my bed, and, behold, *a watcher and a holy one* came down from heaven."

The second occurrence in 4:13 states:

> "The matter is by the decree of *the wat*chers, and the sentence by the word of the holy ones; to the intent that the living may know that the Most High ruleth in the kingdom of men, and giveth it to whomsoever He will, and setteth up over it the lowest of men."

Daniel 4:20 also states:

> "And whereas the king saw *a watcher and a holy one* coming down from heaven, and saying: Hew down the tree, and destroy it; nevertheless leave the stump of the roots thereof in the earth, even in a band of iron and brass, in the tender grass of the field; and let it be wet with the dew of heaven, and

---

[18] 13:3-6. R. H. Charles, *The Book of Enoch* (Oxford: Claredon Press, 1912).

let his portion be with the beasts of the field, till seven times pass over him."

All the occurrences use the singular term *ir* for *watcher* or the plural form *irin* for *watchers*.

As was previously noted, the *Book of Enoch* relates the story of a group of Watchers who descended to earth. They fell from their divine state after they were captivated with mortal women and had intercourse with them.[19] 2 Enoch refers to these Watchers by the Greek transcription *Grigori*.[20] I Enoch[21] and various pseudepigraphical works connect the fall of the angels with the Great Flood.

The progeny of these divine-mortal unions created chaos and violence in the earth. The fallen angels also transmitted knowledge to their wives, which corrupted humanity and the earth.[22] Two fallen angels Shemyaza/Shemihazah and Azazel, are specially pointed out as

---

[19] 1 Enoch 7:2

[20] Andrei A. Orlov, *Dark Mirrors: Azazel and Satanael in Early Jewish Demonology* (New York: SUNY Press, 2011), 164. 2 Enoch 1:3 states: " 3 And they said to me: These are the Grigori, who with their prince Satanail (Satan) rejected the Lord of light, and after them are those who are held in great darkness on the second heaven, and three of them went down on to earth from the Lord's throne, to the place Ermon, and broke through their vows on the shoulder of the hill Ermon and saw the daughters of men how good they are, and took to themselves wives, and befouled the earth with their deeds, who in all times of their age made lawlessness and mixing, and giants are born and marvelous big men and great enmity."

[21] I Enoch 10:4.

[22] I Enoch 10:11–12.

leaders. Azazel is specifically reprimanded by Enoch himself for forbidden teachings.[23]

God sent the **Raphael** to fetter Azazel in the desert Dudael as punishment.[24] Azazel is held responsible for the corruption of the earth. I Enoch 10:8-11 reads:

> "And the whole earth has been corrupted 9 through the works that were taught by Azazel: to him ascribe all sin. And to Gabriel said the Lord: 'Proceed against the bastards and the reprobates, and against the children of fornication: and destroy [the children of fornication and] the children of the Watchers from amongst men [and cause them to go forth]: send them one against the other that they may destroy each other in 10 battle: for the length of days shall they not have. And no request that they (i.e., their fathers) make of thee shall be granted unto their fathers on their behalf; for they hope to live an eternal life and 11 that each one of them will live five hundred years.'"

In 2 Enoch, the story of the fallen angels is altered, with 29:3-4 relating that,

> "3 And one from out the order of angels, having turned away with the order that was under him, conceived an impossible thought, to place his throne higher than the clouds above the earth, that he might become equal in rank to my power.4 And

---

[23] I Enoch 13:1.
[24] I Enoch 10:6.

I threw him out from the height with his angels, and he was flying in the air continuously above the bottomless."

Sefer Hekhahlot or 3 Enoch mentions three fallen angels named Azazel, Azza, and Uzza. They taught witchcraft on earth and caused corruption.[25]

"(7) And what did the generation of Enosh do? They went from one end of the world to the other, and each one brought silver, gold, precious stones, and pearls in heaps like unto mountains and hills, making idols out of them throughout all the world. *And they erected the idols in every quarter of the world*: the size of each idol was 1000 parasangs.
(8) And they brought down the sun, the moon, planets, and constellations, and placed them before the idols on their right hand and on their left, to attend them even as they attend the Holy One, blessed be He, as it is written (1 Kings xxii. 19): 'And all the host of heaven was standing by him on his right hand and on his left.'
(9) What power was in them that they were able to bring them down? They would not have been able to bring them down but for 'Uzza, 'Azza, and 'Azziel, who taught them sorceries whereby they brought them down and made use of them.

---

[25] Annette Yoshiko Reed, *Fallen Angels and the History of Judaism and Christianity: The Reception of Enochic Literature* (Cambridge: Cambridge University Press, 2005), 2 56.

(10) In that time, the ministering angels brought charges (against them) before the Holy One, blessed be He, saying before him: 'Master of the World! What hast thou to do with the children of men?' As it is written (Ps. viii. 4), 'What is man (Enosh) that thou art mindful of him?' 'Mah Adam' is not written here, but 'Mah Enosh,' for he (Enosh) is the head of the idol worshippers.'"

Despite this, they appear in heaven, protesting the presence of Enoch in *Sefer Hekhalot*.[26] The *Book of Jubilees* also refers to the Watchers. They were a class of angels who, along with others, were created on the first day.

"For on the first day He created the heavens which are above and the earth and the waters and all the spirits which serve before him -the angels of the presence, and the angels of sanctification, and the angels [of the spirit of fire and the angels] of the spirit of the winds, and the angels of the spirit of the clouds, and of darkness, and of snow and of hail and of hoar frost, and the angels of the voices and of the thunder and of the lightning, and the angels of the spirits of cold and of heat, and of winter and of spring and of autumn and of summer and of all the spirits of his creatures which are in the heavens and on the earth, (He created) the abysses and the darkness, eventide <and night>, and the light, dawn and day, which

---

[26] 3 Enoch 4:6.

He hath prepared in the knowledge of his heart."[27]

In contrast to the *I Enoch*, the Watchers were initially commanded by God to descend to earth and teach humanity.[28] Like I Enoch, it is only after they cohabited with human women that they violated the boundaries. These illegitimate unions created the giants. The Giants ultimately battled each other until they perished. The Watchers were bound in the depths of the earth as a consequence of their sins. In the *Book of Jubilees,* the fallen angel, Mastema, makes a unique request.

> "And the chief of the spirits, Mastêmâ, came and said: Lord, Creator, let some of them remain before me, and let them harken to my voice, and do all that I shall say unto them; for if some of them are not left to me, I shall not be able to execute the power of my will on the sons of men; for these are for corruption and leading astray before my judgment, for great is the wickedness of the sons of men.'"[29]

In the *Book of Jubilees*, the fallen angels and demons appear to have no authority autonomous from God. They act only on God's plan.[30]

---

[27] *Book of Jubilees* 2:2.
[28] *Book of Jubilees* 1:6.
[29] *Book of Jubilees* 10:1.
[30] Todd R. Hanneken, *The Subversion of the Apocalypses in the Book of Jubilees* (Atlanta: Society of Biblical Literature, 2012), 60.

Some rabbis from the second century forwards rejected Enochic literature. Part of this may have been to prevent Jews from worshiping exalted angels. It may have also explicitly targeted emerging Christian traditions about fallen angels in I and II Peter and the Book of Jude.[31] More significantly, they may have also been targeting the Son of Man imagery in I Enoch, which the Christian movement adopted and ascribing this to Jesus. Daniel Boyarin opines that,

> "...the Gospel text is evidence that these religious ideas were present among Jews in the first century and are being first named and excluded as heresy in the rabbinic text, in other words, that there is no a priori reason to regard this as heresy in the first century at all before the Talmudic intervention. Do not worship a second God as (many of) you have been accustomed to doing so far is the burden of the Talmudic narration of the interaction with the *min*."[32]

Rabbi Simeon bar Yohai was the most pronounced in his opposition to the notion of fallen angels. He went as

---

[31] "While scholars have traditionally sought to study Judaism and Christianity in antiquity by separating and isolating aspects of each religion. It is clear that memorable stories like the ones associated with the Watchers moved easily among religious communities." Angela Kim Harkins, Kelley Coblentz Bautch, and John C. Endres, eds., *The Watchers in Jewish and Christian Traditions* (Minneapolis: Fortress Press, 2014), 1.

[32] Daniel Boyarin, "Beyond Judaisms: Metatron and the Divine Polymorphy of Ancient Judaism," Journal for the Study of Judaism 41 (2010):333.

far as to pronounce a curse against anyone who explained Genesis 6 as interpreting the Sons of God as angels. Rabbi Simeon ben Yohai argued that the Sons of God were sons of judges or sons of nobles. Just as significant was the idea that evil was the result of human inclination.

The idea that the Watchers were fallen angels was almost universal during the Second Temple era, but there were exceptions. The *Sibylline Oracles,* possibly written near the turn of the first century C.E., records a different view, which may have paralleled later rabbinic hesitancy to adopt the seemingly normative view. The Sibylline Oracles relate,

> "These were concerned with fair deeds, noble pursuits, proud honor, and shrewd wisdom. They practiced skills of all kinds, discovering inventions by their needs. One discovered how to till the earth with plows, another carpentry, another was concerned with sailing, another, astronomy and divination by birds, another medicine, again another, magic. Different ones devised that with which they were each concerned, enterprising Watchers, who received this appellation because they had a sleepless mind in their hearts and an insatiable personality. They were mighty, of great form, but nevertheless, they went under the dread house of Tartarus guarded by unbreakable bonds

to make retribution, to Gehenna of terrible raging, undying fire. (1.88-103)" [33]

According to this view, the Watchers were a second generation of humanity, which was curious and inventive. Their advances were initially positive, but magic and divination eventually appeared. As a consequence, they now suffer imprisonment in the netherworld.

The fallen angels were not affected by the flood. Since they are spiritual beings, they cannot be killed. They were imprisoned and wait for their eternal punishment.[34] The most significant element is the evil that is produced through the actions of the fallen angels and the notion that evil was intensified beyond anything that humans had produced to that point. As I Enoch 8:2-3 states:

"And there arose much godlessness, and they committed fornication, and they 3 were led astray, and became corrupt in all their ways."[35]

---

[33] James C. VanderKam, *Enoch: A Man for All Generations* (Columbia: University of South Carolina, 1995), 42. Ibid., 147-148.

[34] James C. VanderKam, *Enoch: A Man for All Generations* (Columbia: University of South Carolina, 1995), 42.

[35] David Suter provides an interesting interpretation to I Enoch 8:1-2. He argues that this section is an allusion to Greek mythology and suggests that fallen angels represents impure priests. The priests were generally teachers and Suter theorizes the critique targeted the Jerusalem priests that introduced Hellenism. David Suter, "Fallen Angel, Fallen Priest: The Problem of Family Purity in 1 Enoch 6-16," HUCA 50 (1979): 115, 132-133. Chris Seeman

---

sees the translation into Greek as renewing contact with eastern and western mythological traditions. Chris Seeman, "The Watchers Traditions and Gen 6:1-4 (MT and LXX)," in Angela Kim Harkins, Kelley Coblentz Bautch, and John C. Endres, eds., *The Watchers in Jewish and Christian Traditions* (Minneapolis: Fortress Press, 2014), 36.

CHAPTER 13

The Rise of Enochic Judaism

Enochic literature, in its various forms, found resonance and acceptance among many in the Second Temple period. That fact is partially connected to the Zadokite priesthood's emergence following the aftermath of the Babylonian exile. Ida Frohlich notes several vital elements that highlight the Babylonian connection to the Enoch tradition.

"The author(s) of the Enochic story in the Book of the Watchers consciously use Mesopotamian lore to theorize about the origins of evil. The bearers of evil and impurity are demonic beings, the offspring of the Watchers. For the author and audience, demons are working in world history. The story of the Watchers (1 En. 6-11) was written following the Babylonian exile. The *terminus ad quem* is the end of the third century BCE. Its language is Aramaic, the vernacular of Mesopotamia and the *lingua franca* of the exiled Judeans from the sixth century BCE."[1]

The centrality of the Torah was mostly undisputed by the early Second Temple period. Commenting on this, Andrei Orlov notes:

"It hardly needs saying that Moses' story, and especially the revelation given to the prophet on Mount Sinai, plays a paramount role in the biblical text posited there as the climatic, formative even responsible for shaping Israel's identity, worship, ethical code, and his social and religious institutions. In the conceptual framework of the Hebrew Bible, it is difficult, perhaps impossible to find a more significant theological disclosure than the reception of the covenantal law in the wilderness."[2]

Despite this, the significant gains made by the Zadokite circles in establishing their dominance in the Jerusalem cult after the exile, their monopoly did not remain unchallenged. More importantly, the Torah does not appear as a central theme of Enochic literature. As James Vanderkam explains, "an attentive reader of I Enoch

---

[1] Ida Frohlich, "Mesoptamian Elements and the Watchers Traditions," in Angela Kim Harkins, Kelley Coblentz Bautch, and John C. Endres, eds., *The Watchers in Jewish and Christian Traditions* (Minneapolis: Fortress Press, 2014), 20.

[2] Andrei A. Orlov, *From Patriarch to the Youth: The Metatron Tradition in 2 Enoch,* PhD diss. (Milwaukee: Marquette University, 2004), 336.

soon becomes aware of the Law of Moses plays almost no role in the book."³ That is not to say that allusions to the Torah do not exist.⁴ I Enoch 9:6 makes it undoubtedly clear that the Torah is being referred to when it states:

"6 And after that in the fourth week, at its close,
Visions of the holy and righteous shall be seen,
And a law for all generations and an enclosure shall be made for them."⁵

I Enoch 89:30-33 relates the Israelites' journey to Mount Sinai and their encounter with God.

---

³ James Vanderkam, "The Interpretation of Genesis I Enoch," in The Bible at Qumran, eds. P. W. Flint and T. H. Kim (Grand Rapids: Eerdmans, 2000), 142.

⁴ James Vanderkam nevertheless suggests that the allusions to the Torah are unclear. He states that "the law is mentioned elsewhere in I Enoch e.g. 5:4; 63:12 seems to be referring to a different [than Mosaic] law; law is used several times for the course of luminaries in chaps. 72-82 [e.g. 79:1-2]; 99:2 speaks of sinners who 'distort the eternal law' but it is not clear what his law is [cf. 104:10]; 108:1 mentions those who 'keep the law in the last days.' But the law is never identified as the law of Moses (or something of the sort); a more common usage of the term is for the laws of nature. This is astounding when one considers how important the judgment is in I Enoch and how often the writers speak of the righteous, doing what is upright, etc. The Torah is also never mentioned in 2 Enoch." www.st-andrews.ac.uk/divinity/rt/otp/bibliog/dmf/enochlit/

⁵ I Enoch via the *Apocalypse of Weeks* and the *Animal Apocalypse* also include allusions to Israel's journey in the wilderness and its acceptance of the Torah.

"And that 30 sheep ascended to the summit of that lofty rock, and the Lord of the sheep sent it to them. And after that, I saw the Lord of the sheep who stood before them, and His appearance was great, and 31 terrible and majestic, and all those sheep saw Him and were afraid before His face. And they all feared and trembled because of Him, and they cried to that sheep with them [which was amongst 32 them]: ' We are not able to stand before our Lord or to behold Him.' And that sheep which led them again ascended to the summit of that rock, but the sheep began to be blinded and to wander 33 from the way which he had showed them, but that sheep wot not thereof."

The fact that the Israelites were afraid of God's presence may highlight Enoch's unique status, who ascended into the heavenly court. Ultimately, James Vanderkam believes that Enochic literature is offering an alternative Judaism to the one centered on the Torah of Moses. Daniel Boyarin opines,

"In my view, Mosaic and Enochic Judaism, far from parting ways, became intertwined very early on (if not *ab origine*; this much I will concede), and any challenge that Enochic traditions posed was entirely from within and from something outside of Torah Judaism."[6]

---

[6] Daniel Boyarin, "Beyond Judaisms: Metatron and the Divine Polymorphy of Ancient Judaism," Journal for the Study of Judaism 41 (2010):358.

This Judaism is centered on the events before the flood.⁷ The *Book of Jubilees* provides a partial response to the notion that Enochic literature was unconcerned with the Torah. Jubilees 21:1-10 portrays Enoch as an authority on Torah law and as part of the chain of transmission.

> "(4) For He is the living God, and He is holy and faithful, and He is righteous beyond all, and there is with Him no accepting of (men's) persons and no accepting of gifts; for God is righteous, and executeth judgment on all those who transgress His commandments and despise His covenant.
>
> (5) And do thou, my son, observe His commandments and His ordinances and His judgments, and walk not after the abominations and after the graven images and after the molten images.
>
> (6) And eat no blood at all of animals or cattle, or of any bird which flies in the heaven.
>
> (7) And if thou dost slay a victim as an acceptable peace offering, slay ye it, and pour out its blood upon the altar, and all the fat of the offering offer on the altar with fine flour and the meat offering mingled with oil, with its drink offering -offer

---

⁷ James Vanderkam, "The Interpretation of Genesis I Enoch," in *The Bible at Qumran*, eds. P. W. Flint and T. H. Kim (Grand Rapids: Eerdmans, 2000), 143.

them all together on the altar of burnt offering; it is a sweet savor before the Lord.

(8) And thou wilt offer the fat of the sacrifice of thank offerings on the fire which is upon the altar, and the fat which is on the belly, and all the fat on the inwards and the two kidneys, and all the fat that is upon them, and upon the loins and liver thou shalt remove, together with the kidneys.

(9) And offer all these for a sweet savor acceptable before the Lord, with its meat-offering and with its drink- offering, for a sweet savor, the bread of the offering unto the Lord.

(10) And eat its meat on that day and on the second day, and let not the sun on the second day go down upon it till it is eaten, and let nothing be left over for the third day; for it is not acceptable [for it is not approved] and let it no longer be eaten, and all who eat thereof will bring sin upon themselves; for thus *I have found it written in the books of my forefathers, and in the words of Enoch*, and in the words of Noah."

Philip Alexander opines that,

> "a pre-Sinai figure [i.e., Enoch] as authoritative in such matter potentially significant, since it could suggest a diminution of the importance

of the Sinai revelation and of its mediator Moses."[8]

Philip Alexander also argued that the emphasis of the Enochic tradition was on science and not on Torah. Philip Alexander states:

"The circles which stand behind the Books of Enoch were...proposing an Enochic paradigm for Judaism in opposition to the emerging Mosaic paradigm-a paradigm based primarily on science as opposed to one based primarily based on law. They were innovators; they had taken on board some of the scientific thought of their day and had used it aggressively to promote a new Jewish worldview."[9]

This does not have to be the case, however. Genesis 26:4-5 states:

---

[8] See Book of Jubilees 7:38-39. Philip Alexander opines that "a pre-Sinai figure [i.e. Enoch] as authoritative in such matter potentially significant, since it could suggest a diminution of the importance of the Sinai revelation and of its mediator Moses." Philip Alexander, "From Son of Adam to a Second God: Transformation of the Biblical Enoch," in Biblical Figures Outside the Bible, ed. M. Stone and T. Bergen (Harrisburg: Trinity Press, 1998), 100.

[9] Philip Alexander, "Enoch and the Beginnings of Jewish Interest in Natural Science," in *The Wisdom Texts from Qumran and the Development of Sapiental Thought*, eds. C. Hempel et al., (Leuven: Peeters, 2002), 234.

"...and I will multiply thy seed as the stars of heaven, and will give unto thy seed all these lands; and by thy seed shall all the nations of the earth bless themselves; *because that Abraham hearkened to My voice, and kept My charge, My commandments, My statutes, and My laws.*"

Abraham is credited with knowing the commandments. This has always been seen as a positive element in rabbinic thought. It does not diminish the Sinai experience. To the contrary, it only confirms its importance of the Torah since the revelation of God's law was now extended to all Israel. From the rabbis perspective, Genesis 26:4-5 buttressed the idea that the Torah was eternal. Those who were genuinely righteous would have known the essence of the Torah in written and oral forms.

The ramifications of the science-based Judaism, per Philip Alexander's view, versus the Law-based Judaism, is a rivalry between Enoch and Moses. Various passages in Enochic literature and other sources from the Second Temple era buttress the case that at least some camps saw a competition between the two interpretations of Jewish life.[10] Philip Alexander notes,

---

[10] Philip Alexander, "From Son of Adam to a Second God: Transformation of the Biblical Enoch," in Biblical Figures Outside the Bible, ed. M. Stone and T. Bergen (Harrisburg: Trinity Press, 1998), 110.

> "A powerful subtext can be detected in the Enochic tradition, implying a contrast between Enoch and Moses. Moses, the lawgiver of Israel, was the founder of the Jewish polity. The circles which looked to Enoch as their patron were, at least to some extent, challenging Moses' primacy. We noted earlier the polemical potential of the fact that Enoch lived long before Moses and the Sinai revelation. It has been plausibly argued that late in the Second Temple period the Enochic writings were canonized into five books- A Pentateuch to rival the Five Books of Moses. We found Enoch occasionally cited as a legal authority who pronounced on halakhic matters explicitly covered in the Torah of Moses..."[11]

Andrei Orlov points to how Enoch received his revelation. He received it by ascending to the heavenly realm and encountered the angels and saw God.[12] Enoch is credited with the ability to see God in a way that Moses could not. 2 Enoch 39:8 states:

> "Frightening and dangerous it is to stand before the face of earthly king, terrifying and very dangerous it is, because the will of the king is death and the will of the king is life. How much more terrifying[and dangerous] it is to stand before the face of the King of earthly kings and of the heavenly armies, [the regulator of the living and

---

[11] Ibid., 107-108.
[12] See I Enoch 89:29-31.

of the dead]. Who can endure the endless misery?"[13]

Who can endure the face of God? Only Enoch can do so. In the case of Moses and the children of Israel, God *descends* to communicate with Moses.[14] The account in Deuteronomy 5:4, however, lends credence to the view that Enoch was not unique in this respect, though the encounter is only temporal. Moses notes that,

> "The LORD spoke with you face to face in the mount out of the midst of the fire."

Exodus 33:1 relates that Moses spoke to God, as a man speaks to his friend. Moreover, Philo cites Moses as sharing an element of God's nature. Philo states in his work titled *On Dreams,*

> "And indeed a divine admonition was given in the following terms to Moses: 'Stand thou here with Me,' {102}{#de 5:31.} by which injunction both these things appear to be intimated, first, the fact that the good man is not moved, and secondly, the universal stability of the living God.
> XXXIV. (2.228) For, in real truth, whatever is akin or near to God is appropriated by him, becoming steady and stationary by reason of his

---

[13] Anderson "2 Enoch" 164.
[14] Andrei A. Orlov, *From Patriarch to the Youth: The Metatron Tradition in 2 Enoch,* PhD diss. (Milwaukee: Marquette University, 2004), 341.

unchangeableness; and the mind, being at rest, well knows how great a blessing rest is, and admiring its own beauty, it conceives that either it is assigned to God alone as his, or else to that intermediate nature which is between the mortal and the immortal race; (2.229) at all events, it says, 'And I stood in the midst between the Lord and You,' {103} {#de 10:10.}"[15]

While Orlov's view has some merit, no one saw Enoch's ascent. In contrast, the revelation at Sinai is said to have been revealed to the entire children of Israel, visually and audibly. The *Words of the Luminaries* from Qumran relate the glorious face conferred upon Moses after his meeting with God at Sinai.

> "[…Re]member, please, that all of us are your people. You have lifted us wonderfully [upon the wings of eagles, and you have brought us to you. And like the eagle which watches its nest, circles [over its chicks,] stretches its wings, takes one and carries it upon [its pinions] […] we remain aloof, and one does not count us among the nations. And […] […] You are in our midst, in the column of fire and in the cloud […] […] your [hol]y […] walks in front of us, and your glory is in [our] midst […] […] the face of Moses, [your] serv[ant]…"[16]

---

[15] 2.228. www.earlyjewishwritings.com/text/philo/book21.html
[16] Garcia Martinez and Eibert J. C. Tigchelaar, eds., *The Dead Sea Scrolls Study Editions 2* (Leiden: Brill, 1992), 1008-1009.

Moses' encounter with God had a lasting impact. Exodus 34:29-30 relates,

> "29 And it came to pass, when Moses came down from mount Sinai with the two tables of the testimony in Moses' hand, when he came down from the mount, that Moses knew not that the skin of his face sent forth beams while He talked with him. 30 And when Aaron and all the children of Israel saw Moses, behold, the skin of his face sent forth beams; and they were afraid to come nigh him."[17]

The challenge to Moses' position in the history of Israel was not only contested by Enoch, who was depicted as restoring the fall of Adam. *Deuteronomy Rabbah* 11:3 offers one scene of the contention between Adam and Moses.

> "Adam said to Moses: 'I am greater than you because I have been created in the image of God.' When this? For it is said, 'and God created man in his own image.' (Genesis 1:27). Moses replied to him: "I am far superior to you, for the honor

---

[17] This verse is taken up in *Sefer Hekhalot* 15B when Metatron, the Sar haPanim tells Moses, "Son of Amram, fear not! For already God favors you. Ask what you will with confidence and boldness, for light shines from the skin of your face from one end of the world to the other." Philip Alexander, "3 (Hebrew Apocalypse of) Enoch," in *The Old Testament Pseudepigrapha*, ed., J.H. Charlesworth (New York: Doubleday, 1985), 304.

which was given to you has been taken away from you, as it is said: but man (Adam) abideth not in honor, (Ps. XLIX, 13), but as for me, the radiant countenance which God gave me still remains with me.' Whence? For it is said: 'his eye was not dim, nor his natural force abated.' (Deuteronomy, 34:7)."[18]

Enochic literature questioned the supremacy of the revelation at Sinai; in turn, other sources questioned Enoch's image. Philo of Alexandria, in his work titled *On Abraham 47,* states:

"Enoch is seen as an example of repentance, and a contrast is drawn between him as a 'penitent' who devoted the earlier part of his life to vice but the latter to virtue, and the 'perfect man' who was virtuous from the first."

This view may have become the basis for later rabbinic assessments on Enoch, which questioned those who believed he was taken because of his righteousness.[19] For Philip Alexander, Enoch's importance in certain circles was an assault on Moses's significance, and a

---

[18] H. Freedman and M. Simon, tr., *Midrash Rabbah 10 Vols* (London: Soncino, 1939), 7.173. The Midrash Tadshe 4 with respect to Moses, states, "in the likeness of the creation of the world the Holy One blessed be he performed miracles for Israel when they came out of Egypt...In the beginning: 'and God created man in his image,' and in the desert: 'and Moshe knew not that the skin of his face shone." Adolf Jellinek, *Bet Ha-Midrash*, 3.168.

[19] See Targum Onkelos on Genesis 5:24; Genesis Rabbah 25:1.

counteroffensive was launched by certain quarters. Philip Alexander states:

"A second line of counterattack was to build up the figure of Moses and to attribute to him the same transcendent qualities as Enoch. Thus some claimed that Moses had ascended into heaven, had received heavenly wisdom, now played a cosmic role as a heavenly being, and had been, in some sense, 'deified.' Elements of this process of exalting Moses may be found as earlier as the *Exagoge* of Ezekiel the Tragedian (second century BCE). Philo, as we have already hinted, accords to Moses divine status, which clearly parallels that assigned elsewhere to Enoch, while at the same time he rather denigrates Enoch. 2 Apoc. Bar. 59:5-12 is an instructive case; there God shows Moses ' the measure of fire, the depths of the abyss, the weight of the winds' and so forth, cosmological doctrines closely associated in earlier tradition with Enoch. A similar transference of Enochic roles to Ezra- as Moses *redividus*- is implied in 4 Ezra 14."[20]

---

[20] Philip Alexander, "From Son of Adam to a Second God: Transformation of the Biblical Enoch," in Biblical Figures Outside the Bible, ed. M. Stone and T. Bergen (Harrisburg, Penn.: Trinity Press, 1998), 108-110. The *Exagoge* of Ezekiel 67-90 states: "Moses: I had a vision of a great throne on the top of the mount Sinai and it reached till the folds of heaven. A noble man was sitting on it, with a crown and a large scepter in his left hand. He beckoned to me with his right hand, so I approached and stood before the throne. He gave me the scepter and instructed me to sit

The fundamental question that must be asked, in my opinion, is to what extent was the *Exagoge* and for that matter, many of the elements of the Enochic tradition widespread. Was the average Jew familiar with *Exagoge* or Enochic traditions?

Opposition to the Zadokites

One stream of opposition literature to the Zadokites centered on Enoch's figure, and the literature ascribed to him.[21] Enochic literature comprised the Book of the Watchers, the work referred to as Aramaic Levi, and the Astronomical Book. Because this constituted the most explicit opposition to Zadokite Judaism outside of the Samaritan scene. This dissenting movement is often referred to as Enochic Judaism.

---

on the great throne. Then he gave me a royal crown and got up from the throne. I beheld the whole earth all around and saw beneath the earth and above the heavens. A multitude of stars fell before my knees and I counted them all. They paraded past me like a battalion of men. Then I awoke from my sleep in fear. Raquel: My friend, this is a good sign from God. May I live to see the day when these things are fulfilled. You will establish a great throne, become a judge a leader of men. As for your vision of the whole earth, the world below and that above the heavens-this signifies that you will see what is, what has been and what shall be." Howard Jacobson, *The Exagoge of Ezekiel* (Cambridge: Cambridge University Press, 1982), 54-55.

[21] James C. Vanderkam, *Enoch: A Man for All Generations* (Columbia: University of South Carolina, 1995), 7-8.

Its apocalyptic and mystical motif characterized Enochic Judaism. However, apocalyptic and mystical trends were not limited to the coalescing forces standing in opposition to the priestly establishment. These trends were reflective of other movements as well.[22] The heart of the conflict between the priestly circles in Jerusalem and Enochic circles does not imply that the literature originated in non-priestly circles. As the Zadokite order established itself, it did so to exclude other priestly families or other groups, maintaining completely different theological constructs fostered by each group's worldviews. Enochic Judaism was not a reaction against the Zadokites by outsiders. Instead, it may have reflected the cry of insiders who had lost their legitimacy to the priesthood and been excluded.[23]

Enochic Judaism viewed the origin of evil in the world as having been linked to fallen angels, a theme strongly emphasized and interestingly adopted by early Christianity in the book of Jude in the New Testament and at Qumran. The fallen angel tradition's pervasiveness existed in Babylonian sources of the exilic age and pre-exilic sources from other Near Eastern sources.[24] The Sons of God's story consorting with the daughters of men was consequently part of the Zadokite body of

---

[22] D.S. Russel, *The Method and Message of Jewish Apocalyptic* (Philadelphia: Westminster, 1964), 27.

[23] Gabriele Boccaccini, *Roots of Rabbinic Judaism: An Intellectual History, from Ezekiel to Daniel* (Grand Rapids: Eerdmans, 2002), 99.

[24] A. Kirk Grayson, *Babylonian Historical- Literary Texts* (Toronto: University of Toronto Press, 1975).

literature. Enochic literature emphasized a much more elaborate version of this story. The story of the angels became a tale of cosmic proportions, and the fallen angels were entrenched in a struggle against God as I Enochic relates:

> "And they became pregnant and bore large giants, and their height (was) three thousand cubits. These devoured all the toil of men until men were unable to sustain them. And the giants turned against them in order to devour men. And they began to sin against birds, and against animals, and against reptiles and against fish, and they devoured one another's flesh and drank the blood from it. Then the earth complained about the lawless ones. (7:3-6; note that most of these categories of animals are included within the beings that are to be destroyed in Genesis 6:7)."[25]

As we saw previously, their offspring, the giants or the *Nephilim*, were essentially demigods. Their spirits continued to wreak havoc throughout the world with their evil deeds even after their physical deaths.

What is of critical importance in Enochic cosmology is the idea that through the fall of the angels and the subsequent seduction of man, the world entered a state of decadence. To restore order, a cataclysmic event characterized by the godly intervention was required. The

---

[25] R. H. Charles, *The Book of Enoch* (Oxford: Clarendon Press, 1912).

idea that a new creation was needed implied that the first creation or the first order was disrepair. This theme of the disorder has been argued to reflect something beyond ante-Diluvian order. Enochic literature maintains a view that despite the exiles' return and the limited restoration of sovereignty, the Babylonian exile had not ended.[26]

Such a view stood firmly against the views of the Zadokites. They sought to position themselves as the guardians of an ancient order and its restoration. This may have very well threatened the basis of Zadokite power that depended so much on the world's concept of order and stability. The most striking feature that attacked Zadokite legitimacy was the priestly role attributed to Enoch. Enochic Judaism assumed an older, pre-Aaronite priesthood that disrupted the Zadokite power structure so dependent on the Sinai theophany. Instead of restoring the ancient priesthood, the Zadokites were perceived as imposters in violation of the cosmic order.[27]

---

[26] Michael A. Knibb, *"The Exile in the Literature of the Intertestamental Period,"* HeyJ 17 (1976), 253-272.

[27] Unlike other movements, the adherents of an Enochic worldview do not appear to have separated themselves from the mainstream of society. Current scholarship on the origins of the Enochic literature places it before the division in Jerusalem cult that led to the separation of various parties from the temple during the Maccabean and Hasmonean eras. Gabriele Boccaccini, *Roots of Rabbinic Judaism: An Intellectual History, from Ezekiel to Daniel* (Grand Rapids: Eerdmans, 2002), 92.

Rabbinic Approaches to Enoch

The possible circumvention of Sinai as the critical event of Biblical history and the prophetic and at times messianic role Enoch plays in the Enochic literature likely led to the very different attitude among emerging rabbinic circles that Enoch was not a wholly righteous individual or at the least that Enoch was not taken up to heaven. Nevertheless, the existence of rabbinic views that was very much in consonant with popular renditions of Enoch reveals that a complete dismissal of Enoch legends was not possible as the Biblical text allowed for alternate renderings. A review of rabbinic approaches to the question of Enochic is appropriate in light of the complicated interpretations surrounding Enoch's life.

The Targum Onkelos of Genesis 5:21-24 provides one example of the neutralization of Enoch's life and the uniqueness of the Biblical passage referring to his being taken up by God:

> "And Enoch walked in reverence of the Lord for 300 years after he begot Methuselah, and he begot sons and daughters. Now all the days of Enoch were 365 ears. And Enoch walked in reverence of the Lord, then he was no more, for the Lord has caused him to die." [28]

---

[28] Bernard Grossfeld, *The Targum Onqelos to Genesis. Aramaic Bible 6* (Wilmington: Michael Glazier, 1988). I was privileged to study with Rabbi Grossfeld at the Spertus Institute of Jewish Learning and Leadership.

Onkelos eliminates Enoch's ascension to God and consequently preserves the uniqueness of the Moses' encounter with God on Sinai and the ascension of Elijah on the fiery chariot.[29] Philo even goes as far as to assign the title god to Moses. In his work *De Vita Mosis 1.158-9*:

> "For he [Moses] was named god and king of the whole nation, and entered, we are told, into the darkness where God was, that is into the unseen, invisible, incorporeal and archetypal essence of existing things. Thus he beheld what is hidden from the sight of mortal nature, and, in himself and his life displayed for all to see, he has set before us, like some well-wrought picture, a piece of work beautiful and godlike, a model for those who are willing to copy it. Happy are those who

---

[29] Philo's *Quaestiones et Solutiones* in Exodum 2.46 preserves a tradition that identifies Moses with the heavenly man created on the seventh day. "But the calling above of the prophet is a second birth better than the first…For he is called on the seventh day, in this (respect) differing from the earth-born first molded man, for the latter came into being from the earth and with body, while the former (came) from the ether and without body. Wherefore the most appropriate number, six, was assigned to the earth-born man, while to the one differently born (was assigned) the higher nature of the hebdomad." R. Marcus, trans., *Philo, Questions and Answers on Exodus* (London: Harvard University Press, 1949), 91-92. Wayne Meeks comments that for Philo "Moses is far superior to the Patriarchs; they had to be initiated into the holy secrets as novices, while Moses officiates from the beginnings as the mystagogue." Wayne A. Meeks, *The Prophet-King: Moses Traditions and the Johannine Christology* (Eugene: Wipf and Stock, 2017), 102.

imprint or strive to imprint, that image in their souls. For it were best that the mind should carry the form of virtue in perfection, but, failing this, let is at least have the unflinching desire to possess that form."[30]

Philo continues in *De Vita Mosis 2:288-91* describing the death of Moses.

"Afterwards the time came when he had to make his pilgrimage from earth to heaven, and leave this mortal life for immortality, summoned thither by the Father who resolved his twofold nature for soul and body into a single unity, transforming his whole being into mind, pure as the sunlight…for when he was already being exalted and stood at the very barrier, ready at the signal to direct his upward flight to heaven, the divine spirit fell upon him, and he prophesied with discernment while still alive the story of his own death."

Rabbinic thought is not absent of views that preserve Enoch's legendary assumption to heaven, however. The Targum Neofiti of Genesis 5:21-24 states:

"And Enoch served in truth before the Lord after he had begotten Methuselah for three hundred years, and during these years he begot sons and daughters. And all the days of the life of Enoch were three hundred and sixty-five years. And Enoch served in truth before the Lord, and it is not

---

[30] F.H. Colson and G.H. Whitaker, trans., *Philo 10 Vols.* (Cambridge: Harvard University Press, 1929), 6.357-59.

known where he is because he was withdrawn by a command from before the Lord."[31]

The figure of Enochic reveals both the interaction and awareness of ancient traditions of the Near Eastern world by the biblical authors. Most interesting perhaps is the careful authoring of the text (especially concerning the *Nephilim*), which effectively allows for views supporting and opposing a particular translation to exist.

The familiarization of Near Eastern myths by the biblical authors also reveals their alteration and reformulation of these figures and stories to fit the emerging mold of their Israelite view of theology and the unique individuals, which led to the rise of the patriarchal line of Abraham.

Philo of Alexandria on Enoch

While most sources viewed Enoch as a righteous individual, Philo of Alexandria provides at least a possible explanation for why later Jewish sources questioned whether Enoch was removed from earth because of righteousness. In his essay titled *On Abraham*, Philo discussed Enosh as a symbol of hope and then turns to Enoch.

---

[31] F.H. Colson and G.H. Whitaker, trans., *Philo 10 Vols.* (Cambridge: Harvard University Press, 1929), 6.593-5. See also M. McNamara, *Targum Neofiti 1: Genesis. Aramaic Bible 1A,* (Collegeville: Liturgical Press, 1992).

"The second place after hope is given to repentance for sins and to improvement, and, therefore, Moses mentions next in order him who changed from the worse life to the better, called by the Hebrew Enoch but in our language 'recipient of grace.' We are told of him that he proved 'to be pleasing to God and was not found because God transferred him,' for transference implies turning and changing, and the change is to the better because it is brought about by the forethought of God. For all that is done with God's help is excellent and truly profitable, as also all that has not His directing care is unprofitable. And the expression used of the transferred person, that he was not found, is well said, either because the old reprehensible life is blotted out and disappears and is no more found, as though it had never been at all, or because he who is thus transferred and takes his place in the better class is naturally hard to find. For evil is widely spread and therefore known to many, while virtue is are, so that even the few cannot comprehend it."[32]

Genesis Rabbah on Enoch relates the following:

"And Enoch walked with God, and he was not; for God took him (v, 24). Rabbi Hama ben Rabbi Hoshaya said: [And he was not means] that he was not inscribed in the scroll of the righteous but

---

[32] James C. Vanderkam, *Enoch: A Man for All Generations* (Columbia: University of South Carolina, 1995), 150-151.

in the scroll of the wicked. Rabbi Aibu said: Enoch was a hypocrite, acting sometimes as a righteous, sometimes as a wicked man. Therefore the Holy One, blessed be He, said: 'While he is righteous, I will remove him/ 1 Rabbi Aibu also said: He judged [i.e., condemned] him on New Year, 2 when he judges the whole world.

Some sectarians 3 asked Rabbi Abbahu: 'We do not find that Enoch died?' 'How so?' inquired he. 'Taking' is employed here, and also in connection with Elijah/ 4 said they. 'If you stress the word 'taking' he answered, 'then 'taking' is employed here, while in Ezekiel it is said, Behold, I take away from thee the desire of thine eyes, etc. (Ezekiel xxiv, 16). 5 Rabbi Tanhuma observed: He answered them well.

A matron asked Rabbi Jose: 'We do not find death stated of Enoch?' Said he to her: 'If it said, And Enoch walked with God, and no more, I would agree with you. Since, however, it says, And he was not, for God took him, it means that he was no more in the world, [having died,] For God took him.'"

The Targumim on Enoch

The official Targum Onkelos renders the Genesis 22-24 in a strikingly different way than expected and refers to Enoch's death. However, two other versions of the

Targum Onkelos include the following alternate phrase, "For the Lord *did not* cause him to die."

The Targum Neofiti provides a more conventional translation of the Hebrew text. Targum Neofiti states:

> "22 And Enoch served in truth before the Lord after he had begotten Methuselah for three hundred years, and during these years he begot sons and daughters. 23 And all the days of the life of Enoch were three hundred and sixty-five years. 24 And Enoch served in truth before the Lord, and it is not known where he is, because he was withdrawn by a command from before the Lord."[33]

The Targum Pseudo-Jonathan is the boldest in its application of later Enoch lore to Genesis 5. The Targum reads:

> "22 Enoch worshiped in truth before the Lord after he had begotten Methuselah three hundred years, and he begot sons and daughters. 23 All the days of Enoch with the inhabitants of the earth were three hundred and sixty-five years. 23 Enoch worshiped in truth before the Lord and behold he was not with the inhabitants of the earth because he was taken away, and he ascended to

---

[33] James C. Vanderkam, *Enoch: A Man for All Generations* (Columbia: University of South Carolina, 1995), 166.

the firmament at the command of the Lord, and he was called Metatron, the Great Scribe."[34]

Regarding Metatron, Philip Alexander writes:

"Metatron is, in a number of respects, similar to the archangel Michael: Both angels were known as 'the Great Prince'; both were said to serve in the heavenly sanctuary; both were guardian angels of Israel; what is said in one text about Michael is said in another about Metatron. A possible explanation of these similarities would be that originally Metatron and Michael were one and the same angel; Michael was the angel's common name, Metatron, one of his esoteric, magical names. At some point, however, the connection between Metatron and Michael was obscured, and a new, independent archangel with many of Michael's powers came into being...Metatron was merged with two other heavenly figures, (1) the archangel Yaho'el, and (2) translated Enoch...Metatron's absorption of translated Enoch could only have taken place in circles acquainted with the Palestinian apocalyptic Enoch traditions. The apocalyptic texts do not seem to go so far as to say that Enoch was transformed into an archangel when he was translated into heaven, but some of them speak of his exaltation

---

[34] Ibid., 167.

in language, which could be taken to imply this (see esp. 2 En. 22:8).[35]

---

[35] Philip Alexander, "3 (Hebrew Apocalypse of) Enoch," in *The Old Testament Pseudepigrapha*, ed., J.H. Charlesworth (New York: Doubleday, 1985), 1.243-44. James C. Vanderkam, *Enoch: A Man for All Generations* (Columbia: University of South Carolina, 1995), 168.

CHAPTER 14

Enoch and the New Testament

The New Testament includes several references to Enoch, but the impact of Enochic literature goes far beyond these limited citations. Jesus is assigned titles and roles which, at the minimum, parallel those attributed to Enoch. Jesus describes himself as a prophet (seer) and is also designated as one by others.[1] He is described as a high priest.[2] He is a knower of secrets.[3] Jesus is the revealer of mysteries.[4] In the book of Hebrews, he is described as greater than Moses.[5] He describes himself as the Son of Man more than eighty times in the Gospels.[6] He is designated as the Chosen or

---

[1] Matthew 21:11, 21:46; Mark 6:4; Luke 4:24, 7:16, 9:8, 9:19; John 4:19, 6:14, 7:40; Acts 3:22, 7:37.
[2] Hebrews 6:20; 7:24-26;
[3] Matthew 12:25; Luke 5:22, 11:17.
[4] Matthew 13:11; Ephesians 1:9.
[5] Hebrews 3:3.
[6] See Larry W. Hurtado, *Lord Jesus Christ: Devotion to Jesus in Earliest Christianity* (Grand Rapids: Wm B. Eerdmans Publishing Co., 2005) 290-293.

Elect one of God.[7] The parallels may seem too coincidental to quickly dismiss the view that the Enoch tradition influenced the Jesus movement. As I outlined in *Forgotten Origins: The Lost Jewish History of Early Christianity*, there were many early Christian streams. The evolution of "Jesus theology" did not necessarily reflect uniform developments or outcomes. What may have been accepted by one group of Jews who supported Jesus' messianic claims may not have been accepted by others.

There are other connections between the Enoch tradition and early Christianity. A central core of Jesus' activity includes exorcisms. There is, however, no explanation in the Gospels for the ubiquitous presence of demons. Their existence is assumed as a matter of fact despite the relative silence of the Hebrew Bible on the topic. The existence of demons requires a back story and the Enoch tradition likely provided the background.

The New Testament adopts the character of Satan or the Adversary as God's principal opponent. Despite the importance of Satan, his fall from Heaven evokes the imagery of punishment given to the *Fallen Watchers*. Annette Yoshiko Reed explains the complicated relationship with the Watcher tradition.

> "Despite the many changes in the centuries between the composition of the Book of the Watchers and the rise of the Jesus Movement, the

---

[7] John 1:34; Luke 23"35; 1 Peter 2:4-6.

patterns in the use of the Enochic myth of angelic descent remained surprisingly stable. Many exegetes seem to have read Gen 6:1-4 through 1 En. 6-16. With very few exceptions, however, Jewish and Christian texts from this period omit references to illicit angelic instruction, focus on the Watchers' sexual sins, and downplay or reject the Book of Watcher's assertion that angelic descent accounts for the origins of human sin and suffering."[8]

The Significance of Enoch

Enoch's importance to various circles of Jewish Jesus followers is confirmed in multiple passages in the New Testament. The epistle of Jude 14-15, for example, states:

"[14] And Enoch also, the seventh from Adam, prophesied of these, saying, Behold, the Lord cometh with ten thousands of his saints,

[15] To execute judgment upon all, and to convince all that are ungodly among them of all their ungodly deeds which they have ungodly committed,

---

[8] Annette Yoshiko Reed, *Fallen Angels and the History of Judaism and Christianity* (Cambridge: Cambridge Press, 2004), 86.

and of all their hard speeches which ungodly sinners have spoken against him."[9]

Whether Jude is the brother of Jesus and James is not important, considering that this short epistle attributes veracity to the *Book of Enoch*.[10] The early Christian movement, or at least one strata of it, affirmed Enoch's importance but opted to transfer the messianic titles assigned to the former to Jesus. For this group of Jewish supporters of Jesus, the *Book of Enoch* was correct in its fundamental assertion that evil had entered the world through the Watchers' great sin. This is verified by 2 Peter 2:4-6, which states:

"4 For if God spared not the angels that sinned, but cast them down to hell, and delivered them into chains of darkness, to be reserved unto judgment;

5 And spared not the old world, but saved Noah the eighth person, a preacher of righteousness,

---

[9] The Enochic tradition was apparently accepted by Irenaeus as part of prophetic tradition. See *Adversus Haereses 1.10.1*. For the complexity of the concept of Scripture in early Christianity, see J. Barr, *Holy Scripture: Canon, Authority, Criticism* (Philadelphia: West- minster, 1983), 55 and Annette Yoshiko Reed, *Fallen Angels and the History of Judaism and Christianity* (Cambridge: Cambridge Press, 2004), 155, 156.

[10] Hebrews 11:5 supports the view that Enoch was righteous. "*5* By faith Enoch was translated that he should not see death; and was not found, because God had translated him: for before his translation he had this testimony, that he pleased God."

bringing in the flood upon the world of the ungodly;

6 And turning the cities of Sodom and Gomorrah into ashes condemned them with an overthrow, making them an example unto those that after should live ungodly;"

I Peter 3:18-20 also refers to Jesus' journey to the spirits that were imprisoned, though their identity is not fully established.

"18 For Christ also hath once suffered for sins, the just for the unjust, that he might bring us to God, being put to death in the flesh, but quickened by the Spirit:

19 By which also he went and preached unto the spirits in prison;

20 Which sometime were disobedient, when once the longsuffering of God waited in the days of Noah, while the ark was a preparing, wherein few, that is, eight souls were saved by water."

Who the imprisoned spirits were is not stated, but this may be drawn from Enoch's encounter with the *Fallen Watchers,* who pleaded with him to intercede on their behalf. Annette Yoshiko Reed points to Irenaeus' *Adversus Haereses 1.10.1*. In this passage, Irenaeus contends that Jesus will carry out judgment on the fallen angels and wicked humans at the End of Time. Reed suggests that in contrast to I Peter, Irenaeus focuses on the eschatological judgment. In the *Book of Watchers,* this role is undertaken by God. For Irenaeus, this role is transferred to Jesus. The position stands in contrast to I Peter, which echoed Enoch's role in the Book of Watchers before the Flood.[11] The critical point of distinction was that Jesus, and not Enoch was the redeeming figure. Paul's reference to Jesus as the second Adam in I Corinthians 15:45 may have been an inspiration for other Christian circles. They may have adopted the idea of Jesus as the second Enoch.

Early Christianity in the second century CE, as reflected by the Church Father Justin, accepted the premise that some Watchers had fallen and mixed with human women. In his *Second Apology,* Chapter 5, Justin states:

> "But if this idea takes possession of someone, that if we acknowledge God as our helper, we should not, as we say, be oppressed and persecuted by the wicked; this, too, I will solve. God, when He had made the whole world, and subjected things earthly to man, and arranged the heavenly elements for the increase of fruits and rotation of the seasons, and appointed this divine law — for these things also He evidently made for man — committed the care of men and of all things under heaven to angels whom He appointed over them. *But the angels transgressed this appointment, and were captivated by love of women, and begot children who are those that are called demons*; and besides, they afterward subdued the human

---
[11] Ibid., 150.

race to themselves, partly by magical writings, and partly by fears and the punishments they occasioned, and partly by teaching them to offer sacrifices, and incense, and libations, of which things they stood in need after they were enslaved by lustful passions; and among men, they sowed murders, wars, adulteries, intemperate deeds, and all wickedness. Whence also the poets and mythologists, not knowing that it was the angels and those demons who had been begotten by them that did these things to men, and women, and cities, and nations, which they related, ascribed them to god himself, and to those who were accounted to be his very offspring, and to the offspring of those who were called his brothers, Neptune and Pluto, and to the children again of these their offspring. For whatever name each of the angels had given to himself and his children, by that name, they called them."[12]

Many Church Fathers accepted the Watcher tradition. The messianic titles ascribed to Enoch do not appear to have been an issue. Annette Yoshiko Reed notes that,

"Even though ecclesiarchs in the Roman Empire eventually followed their Rabbinic counterparts in formulating alternative approaches to Gen 6:1-4, we find no evidence that the angelic interpretation of Gen 6:1-4 was a 'marginal' or 'heretical'

---

[12] Annette Yoshiko Reed, *Fallen Angels and the History of Judaism and Christianity* (Cambridge: Cambridge Press, 2004), 149.

position in the second and third centuries. In fact, this view is propounded by some of the most influential proto-orthodox writers of the time, including Justin Martyr, Tatian, Irenaeus, Clement of Alexandria, Bardaisan, Tertullian, Commodian, Cyprian, and Lactantius."[13]

Interestingly, the Church's acceptance of the *Fallen Watchers* tradition eventually ended through the influence of the Church Father Augustine.[14]

"Let us omit, then, the fables of those scriptures which are called apocryphal, because their obscure origin was unknown to the fathers from whom the authority of the true Scriptures has been transmitted to us by a most certain and well-ascertained succession. For though there is some truth in these apocryphal writings, yet they contain so many false statements, that they have no canonical authority. We cannot deny that Enoch, the seventh from Adam, left some divine writings, for this is

---

[13] Ibid., 149.

[14] The Church Father Tertullian (circa 160-220 CE) noted that the Enochic tradition was not accepted in all Christian circles. In his work titled *De cultu feminarum* 1.2 Tertullian states: "I am aware that the Scripture of Enoch, which has assigned this order [of action] to angels, is not received by some, because it is not admitted into the Jewish canon [lit. chest; i.e., ark of the Torah?]." The Church Father Origen, circa 184 -253 CE, questioned the canonical status of Enoch because it was not accepted among Jews. Annette Yoshiko Reed, *Fallen Angels and the History of Judaism and Christianity* (Cambridge: Cambridge Press, 2004), 195, 198.

asserted by the Apostle Jude in his canonical epistle. But it is not without reason that these writings have no place in that canon of Scripture which was preserved in the temple of the Hebrew people by the diligence of successive priests; for their antiquity brought them under suspicion, and it was impossible to ascertain whether these were his genuine writings, and they were not brought forward as genuine by the persons who were found to have carefully preserved the canonical books by a successive transmission."[15]

Oddly enough, the fact that emerging rabbinic circles had not included the Enoch tradition as Scripture was one factor in Augustine's decision. As Christianity matured, the theological implications of accepting the Enochic tradition may have become apparent. As was demonstrated in chapter ten, the *Book of Enoch* provides messianic imagery and titles, including the Son of Man, which is extensively used in the New Testament and applied to Jesus. For all of the benefits it may have provided in setting the early Christian movement stage as an authentic Jewish expression, the *Book of Enoch* designated Enoch and not Jesus as *the* Chosen One. The Chosen or Elect one's elevated status in the Enoch tradition certainly provided Christianity with a foundation to draw from. Still, it was not a seamless connection nor one that resolved objections to it.

---

[15] Augustine, *The City of God Book XV, Chapter 23.* http://www.newadvent.org/fathers/120115.htm

On the matter of Jesus' exalted status in early Christianity, Daniel Boyarin seems to admit the challenges of this perspective even in light of Enochic tradition. He states:

> "This suggests to me that in their project of producing an orthodoxy for Judaism, the Rabbis were disowning a common (how common, I think, we will never know) Jewish practice of worship of the second God, actually named within mystical texts, the lesser YHWH [My name is in him), Metatron, who is Enoch, the Son of Man."[16]

Of course, the problem lies in the fact that the Gospel of John (10:33) states there was clear opposition to the direct or indirect suggestion that divine status was applied to a man. Assuming the Gospel of John was written at the end of the first century C.E. or even as late as 120 C.E., it is, I believe, reasonable to consider that while the other Gospels proclaimed the Son of Man imagery and applied this to Jesus, John goes the farthest in ascribing full divine status if not equivalency.

And therein lies the issue. Daniel Boyarin assumes that the Metatron tradition was "common," though he admits it was found in mystical circles. Mystical circles, almost by default, are selective, small groups that do not necessarily reflect views common to the masses. Who,

---

[16] Daniel Boyarin, "Beyond Judaisms: Metatron and the Divine Polymorphy of Ancient Judaism," Journal for the Study of Judaism 41 (2010): 335.

in short, worshipped Metatron? Magical incantations aside in late antiquity, there does not appear to be a record of this occurring. The response to this question has, as far as I have come across, remained unanswered. This reality should help us consider that while the Enochic tradition contributed to a religious environment that the early Jewish supporters of Jesus may have drawn from, many issues remain unresolved.

The different streams represented in the New Testament and outside of it adapted these ideas and transformed them according to their convictions and beliefs. The concretization of Christology in later Christianity likely created a challenge that most emerging rabbis could not endorse or leave unanswered. It did not surprisingly eliminate the presence of mystical traditions that retained or perhaps even created a parallel stream of elevated angels sharing in God's identity in some form or fashion. These rabbinic groups continued to transmit texts which appear at times as complementary versions of what we so often deem Christianity. The lines between Christianity and Judaism were not as concrete as we often assumed and continued to remain porous for several centuries.

Bibliography

Abrahams, Daniel. "The Boundaries of Divine Ontology: The Inclusion and Exclusion of Metatron in the Godhead," HTR 87 (1994).

Alon, Gedaliah. *Jews, Judaism, and the Classical World*, Trans. I. Abraham. Jerusalem: Magnes, 1977.

Alexander, Philip S. "Targum, Targumim," in the Anchor Bible Dictionary, ed. David Noel Freedman, Gary A Herion, David F. Graf, and John David Pleins. New York: Double Day, 1992.

Amidon, Philip R. *The Panarion of St. Epiphanius, Bishop of Salamis*. Oxford: Oxford University Press, 1990.

Arguiti, Yitzchok Behar *The Torah Anthology Me'am Loez*. New York: Moznaim Publishing, 1984.

Baeck, Leo. *Judaism and Christianity*. Philadelphia: Jewish Publication Society, 1958.

Barclay, John M.G. *Jews in the Mediterranean Diaspora: From Alexandria to Trajan*. Berkley: University of California Press, 1996.

Barth, Frederik ed., *Ethnic Groups and Boundaries: The Social Organization of Cultural Difference*. Bergen: Universitets Forlaget, 1969.

Barnstone, Willis. *The Other Bible*. San Francisco: Harper San Francisco, 1984.

Bauckham, Richard. *The Book of Acts in its Palestinian Setting*. Grand Rapids: Eerdmans, 1995.

Bauckham, Richard. *Jude and the Relatives of Jesus in the Early Church.* Edinburgh: T&T Clark, 1990.

Becking, Bob and Korpel, Marjo C.A. *The Crisis of Israelite Religion.* Boston: Brill, 1999.

Berquist, Jon L. *Judaism in Persia's Shadow: A Social and Historical Approach.* Minneapolis: Fortress Press, 1995.

Bennet, D.M. *Sepher Todoth Jeshu.* New York: Liberal Publisher, 1879.

Bickerman, Elias. *The Jews in the Greek Age.* Cambridge: Harvard, 1988.

Boccaccini, Gabriele. *Roots of Rabbinic Judaism: An Intellectual History, from Ezekiel to Daniel,* Grand Rapids: Eerdmans, 2000.

Bockmuehl, Markus. *Revelation and Mystery in Ancient Judaism and Pauline Christianity.* Grand Rapids: Eerdmans, 1990.

Borgen, Peder. *Early Christianity and Hellenistic Judaism.* Edinburgh: T& T Clark, 1996.

Boyarin, Daniel. "Beyond Judaisms: Metatron and the Divine Polymorphy of Ancient Judaism," Journal for the Study of Judaism 41 (2010):323-365.

Boyarin, Daniel. "The Gospel of the Memra: Jewish Binitarianism and the Prologue to John," The Harvard Theological Review, Vol. 94 No. 3 (2001).

Boyle, Isaac. *Eusebius- The Ecclesiastical History.* Cambridge: Harvard University Press, 1926.

Brandon, S.G.F. *Jesus and the Zealots.* Manchester: The University Press, 1967.

Breiter, Yitchok. *Seven Pillars of Faith & A Day in the Life of a Breslover Chassid.* Monsey: The Breslov Research Institute, 1989.

Buber, Martin. *Two Types of Faith.* New York: Harper Torch Books, 1961.

Burkitt, F.C. *Christian Beginnings.* London: University of London Press, 1924.

Buchholz, Dennis D. *Your Eyes Will be Opened: A Study of the Greek (Ethiopic Apocalypse of Peter).* Atlanta: Scholars Press, 1988.

Chadwick, Henry. *Origen: Contra Celsum.* Cambridge: The Cambridge University Press, 1953.

Charlesworth, James H. *Jesus and the Dead Sea Scrolls.* New York: Doubleday, 1992.

Charlesworth, James. *Jesus' Jewishness: Exploring the Place of Jesus in Early Judaism.* New York: Crossroad Publishing, 1996.

Charles, R.H. *The Book of Enoch.* London; Society for Promotion of Christian Knowledge, 1917.

Chase, Irah trans., *Constitutions of the Holy Apostles.* New York: D. Appleton & Company, 1848.

Chazan, Robert. *From Anti-Judaism to Anti-Semitism: Ancient and Medieval Christian Constructions of Jewish History.* Cambridge: Cambridge University Press, 2016.

Cogan, M.D. "*Canaanite Origins and Lineage: Reflections on the Religion of Ancient Israel,*" in Ancient Israelite Religion: Essays I Honor of F.M. Cross, P.D. Miller. Philadelphia: Fortress, 1987.

Cogan, M.D. *Imperialism and Religion: Assyria, Judah, and Israel in the Eighth and Seventh Centuries B.C.E.* SBLMS 19; Missoula, MT: SBL and Scholars, 1974.

Cohen, Shaye J. D. *The Beginnings of Jewishness: Boundaries, Varieties, Uncertainties.* Berkeley: University of California Press, 2000.

Cohen, Shaye J. D. *From Maccabees to the Mishnah.* Philadelphia: Westminster Press, 1987.

Cohen, Shaye J.D. *Yavneh Revisited: Pharisees, Rabbis, and the End of Jewish Sectarianism.* Chico: Scholars Press: 1982.

Cohn-Sherbok, Dan. *The Crucified Jew: Twenty Centuries of Christian Anti-Semitism.* William B. Eerdmans Publishing Company, 1997.

Collins, J.J. *Seers, Sybils, and Sages in Hellenistic-Roman Judaism SJSJ 54.* Leiden: Brill, 1997.

Evans, Craig A. and Hagner, Donald A. *Anti-Semitism and Early Christianity: Issues of Polemic and Faith.* Minneapolis: Fortress Press, 1993.

Cruse, Christian. *The Ecclesiastical History of Eusebius Pamphilus.* Grand Rapids: Baker Book House, 1992.

Dan, Joseph. *The Ancient Jewish Mysticism.* Tel Aviv, MOD Books, 1993.

Danielou, Jean. *The Theology of Jewish Christianity.* London: Darton, Longman & Todd, 1979.

Davids, Peter H. "James's Message: The Literary Record," in the *Brother of Jesus: James the Just and His Mission,* eds. Bruce Chilton and Jacob Neusner. Louisville: Westminster John Knox Press, 2001.

Davies, Alan T. *Anti-Semitism and the Foundations of Christianity.* Wipf & Stock Publishers, 2004.

Davies, Philip *Scribes and Schools: The Canonization of the Hebrew Scriptures.* Louisville: Knox Press, 1998.

Dimont, Max I. *Jews, God, and History.* New York: The New American Library, Inc., 1962.

Dupont, A. *The Essene Writings from Qumran,* trans. G.Vermes. Oxford, 1961.

Diana Edelman, ed., *The Triumph of Elohim: From Yahwisms to Judaisms.* Grand Rapids: Wm. B. Eerdmans, 1995.

Dever, William G. *What Did the Biblical Writers Know and When did They know it?* Grand Rapids: Eerdmans, 2001.

Eisenman, Robert. *James the Brother of Jesus.* New York: Viking, 1996.

Falk, Harvey. *Jesus the Pharisee: A New Look at the Jewishness of Jesus.* Eugene: Wipf & Stock Publishers, 2003.

Farrar, Fredrick W. *The Early Days of Christianity.* New York: Cassel and Company, 1909.

Feldman, Louis H. *Jewish Life and Thought among Greeks and Romans.* Minneapolis: Fortress Press, 1996.

Fine, Steve. *Jews, Christians, and Poly-Theists in the Ancient Synagogue.* London: Routledge, 1999.

Fishman, Talya. *Early Modern Workshop: The Jewishness of Conversos.* Wesleyan University, 2012.

Fitzmyer, Joseph. *The Acts of the Apostles.* New York: Double Day, 1998.

Flesher, Paul "The Targumim," in Judaism in Late Antiquity, Vol. 1, ed. Jacob Neusner. Boston: Brill Academic Publishers, 2001.

Gager, John G. *The Origins of Anti-Semitism: Attitudes toward Judaism in Pagan and Christian Antiquity.* Oxford: Oxford University Press, 1985.

Garcia Martinez, F. and Tigchelaar, Eibert J.C. (eds.), *The Dead Sea Scrolls Study Edition Volume 1.* Leiden: Brill, 1997.

Glazter, Nahum N. *Hammer on the Rock: A Midrash Reader.* New York: Schocken Books, 1974.

Goldstein, Jonathan. *The Anchor Bible: I Maccabees.* Garden City: Doubleday & Company, Inc, 1976.

Goldstein, Jonathan A. "How the Authors of 1 and 2 Maccabees Treated the 'Messianic' Promises," in the *Judaisms and their Messiahs at the Turn of the Christian Era*, ed. Jacob Neusner. Cambridge: Cambridge University, 1987.

Gottwald, Norman K. *The Tribes of Yahweh.* Maryknoll: Orbis Books, 1979.

Gnuse, Robert Karl. *No Other Gods: Emergent Monotheism in Israel.* Sheffield: Sheffield Academic Press, 1997.

Grelot, Pierre. "La Légende d'Hénoch dans les apocryphes et dans la Bible: son origine et signification" *RSR* 46 (1958) 5-26.

Guetta, Alessandro "Leone Modena's Magen va-Herev as an Anti-Catholic Apologia," Jewish Studies Quarterly, Vol. 7, No. 4 (2000).

Grabbe, Lester *The Samaritans in the Hasmonean Period*, 1999.

Grayson, A. Kirk *Babylonian Historical- Literary Texts*. Toronto: University of Toronto Press, 1975.

Green, William S. "Introduction: Messiah in Judaism: Rethinking the Question," in *the Judaisms and their Messiahs at the Turn of the Christian Era*, ed. Jacob Neusner. Cambridge: Cambridge University, 1987.

Grossfeld, Bernard. *The Targum Onqelos to Genesis, Aramaic Bible 6*. Wilmington: Michael Glazier, 1988.

Raimo Hakola. "The Johannine Community as Jewish Christians? Some Problems in Current Scholarly Consensus," in *Jewish Christianity Reconsidered: Rethinking Ancient Groups and Texts*, ed. Matt Jackson-McCabe. Minneapolis: Fortress Press, 2007.

Halivni, David Weiss. *Revelation Restored: Divine Writ and Critical Responses*. Boulder: Westview: 1997.

Hall III, Sidney G. *Christian Anti-Semitism and Paul's Theology*. Minneapolis: Fortress Press, 1993.

Hannah, Darrell D. *Michael and Christ: Michael Traditions and Angel Christology in Early Christianity* . Tubingen: Mohr Siebeck, 1999.

Hect, Richard "Philo and Messiah," in *the Judaisms and their Messiahs at the Turn of the Christian Era*, ed. Jacob Neusner. Cambridge: Cambridge University, 1987.

Hengel, Martin. *The Zealots*. Edinburg: T&T Clark, 1989.

Herford, R. Travers. *Christianity in Talmud and Midrash*. New York: Ktav, 1903.

Hill, Craig C. "The Jerusalem Church" in *Jewish Christianity Reconsidered: Rethinking Ancient Groups and Texts*, ed. Matt Jackson-McCabe. Minneapolis: Fortress Press, 2007.

Hurtado, Larry W. *One God, One Lord*. Minneapolis: Fortress Press, 1988.

Hurtado, Larry W. *Lord Jesus Christ: Devotion to Jesus in Earliest Christianity* (Grand Rapids: Wm B. Eerdmans Publishing Co., 2005.

Jackson-McCabe, Matt "The Messiah Jesus in the Mythic World of James," JBL 122/4 (2003).

Jackson-McCabe, Matt. "What's in a name? The Problem of 'Jewish Christianity'" in *Jewish Christianity Reconsidered: Rethinking Ancient Groups and Texts*, ed. Matt Jackson-McCabe. Minneapolis: Fortress Press, 2007.

Jagersma, H. *A History of Israel: From Alexander the Great to Bar Kochba*. Philadelphia: Fortress Press, 1986.

Jellinek, A. *Beit Ha-Midrash, Vol. 6.* Jerusalem: Bamberger et Vahrman 1938.

Jocz, Jakob. *The Jewish People and Jesus Christ*. Grand Rapids: Baker Book House, 1949.
Collins, John J. *The Scepter and the Star: The Messiah of the Dead Sea Scrolls and Other Ancient Literature*. New York: Doubleday, 1995.

Katz, Jacob. *Exclusiveness and Tolerance: Studies in Jewish-Gentile Relations in Medieval & Modern Times*. West Orange: Behrman House, 1961.

Kaufmann, Yehezkel. *The Religion of Israel: From its Beginnings to the Babylonian Exile*. New York: Schocken: 1960.

Klausner, Joseph. *Jesus of Nazareth*. New York: The Macmillan Company, 1943.

Klausner, Joseph. *Jesus of Nazareth: His Life, Times, and Teaching*. New York: The Macmillan Company, 1926.

Klausner, Joseph. *From Jesus of Paul.* New York: The Macmillan Company, 1943.

Klijn, A.F.G and Reinink, G.J. *Patristic Evidence for Jewish-Christian Sects.* Leiden: Brill, 1973.

Kraft, R.A.*The Multiform Jewish Heritage of Early Christianity*, in Neusner (ed.). *Christianity, Judaism and Other Greco-Roman Cults: Studies for Morton Smith at Sixty*, ed Jacob Neusner, vol 3. Leiden: Brill, 1975.

Knibb, Michael A. "*The Exile in the Literature of the Intertestamental Period*," Heythrop Journal 17, 1976: 253-272.

Lasor, William S. *The Dead Sea Scrolls and the New Testament.* Grand Rapids: Eerdmans, 1972.

Lee, Bernard J. *The Galilean Jewishness of Jesus.* New York: Paulist Press, 1988.

Leiman, Sid Z. *The Canonization of Hebrew Scripture: The Talmudic and Midrashic Evidence.* Hamden: Archon Books, 1976.

Levine, Lee I. *Judaism and Hellenism in Antiquity: Conflict or Confluence.* Peabody: Hendrickson, 1998.

Levey, Samson H. *The Messiah: An Aramaic Interpretation. The Messianic Exegesis of the Targum.* Cincinnati: Monographs of the Hebrew Union College 2, 1974.

Lewis, Jack P. "The Woman's Seed," JETS 34/3 September (1991).

Luedemann, Gerd. *Opposition to Paul in Jewish Christianity.* Minneapolis: Fortress, 1989.

Luomanen, Petri "Ebionites and Nazarenes'" in *Jewish Christianity Reconsidered: Rethinking Ancient Groups and Texts*, ed. Matt Jackson-McCabe. Minneapolis: Fortress Press, 2007.

Macho, A. D. *Neofiti I*. Madrid: Consejo Superior de Investigaciones Cientificas, 1968.

Marcus, Jacob R. *The Jew in the Medieval World*. Cincinnati: The Sinai press, 1938.

Mazar, Benjamin. *Biblical Israel: State and People*. Jerusalem: Magnes Press, 1992.

Modrzejewski, Joseph Meleze. *The Jews of Egypt: From Ramses II to the Emperor Hadrian*, Edinburgh: T&T Clark, 1995.

Miller, Patrick. *The Religion of Ancient Israel*. London: SPCK, 2000.

Milik, Jazef. T. ed., *The Books of Enoch: Aramaic Fragments of Qumran Cave 4*. Oxford: Oxford, 1976.

Mulder, Martin Jan. *Mikra: Text, Translation, Reading and Interpretation of the Hebrew Bible in Ancient Judaism and in Early Christianity*. Minneapolis: Fortress Press, 1990.

Maccoby, Hyam. *The MythMaker: Paul and the Invention of Christianity*. New York: Barnes and Nobles, 1986.

Nicholls, William. *Christian Antisemitism: A History of Hate*. Jason Aronson, Inc., 1995.

Nickelsburg, W.E. and Vanderkam, James C. *1 Enoch: The Hermeneia Translation*. Minneapolis: Fortress Press, 2012.

Neusner, Jacob. *Judaic Perspectives on Ancient Israel*. Philadelphia: Fortress Press, 1987.

Neusner, Jacob ed., *Judaism in Late Antiquity: Where We Stand: Issues and Debates in Ancient Judaism.* Boston: Brill, 1999.

Neusner, Jacob. *Judaisms and Their Messiahs at the Turn of the Christian Era.* New York: Cambridge, 1987.

Neusner, Jacob. *Rabbinic Judaism: Structure and System.* Minneapolis: Fortress Press, 1995.

Neusner, Jacob. *There We Sat Down.* Hoboken: Ktav, 1978.

Nickelsburg, George W. E. "Salvation without and with a Messiah: Developing Beliefs in Writings Ascribed to Enoch," in the *Judaisms and their Messiahs at the Turn of the Christian Era*, ed. Jacob Neusner. Cambridge: Cambridge University, 1987.

Orlov, Andrei A. *From Patriarch to the Youth: The Metatron Tradition in 2 Enoch,* Ph.D. diss. Milwaukee: Marquette University, 2004.

Orlov, Andrei A. "Titles of Enoch-Metatron in 2 Enoch," Journal for the Study of the Pseudepigrapha 18 (1998).

Orlov, Andrei A. *The Enoch-Metatron Tradition.* Tübingen: Mohr Siebeck, 2005.

Orr, Akiva. *Israel, Politics, Myths and Identity Crisis.* London: Pluto Press, 1994.

Painter, John. *Just James: The Brother of Jesus in History and Tradition.* Columbia: University of South Carolina Press, 1997.

Paget, James Carleton "The Ebionites in Recent Research" in *Jews, Christians and Jewish Christians in Antiquity.* Tubingen: Mohr Siebeck, 2010.

Parkes, James. *The Conflict of the Church and the Synagogue.* New York: Atheneum, 1985.

Patai, Raphael. *The Messiah Texts*. New York: Avon Books, 1979.

Platt, Rutherford H. ed., *The Forgotten Books of Eden*. New York: Alpha House, 1926.

Pearse, Roger. "John Chrysostom, Against the Jews. Homily 1." John Chrysostom, Against the Jews. Homily 1. Accessed February 13, 2017. https://goo.gl/A54nJ8

Pines, Shlomo. *The Jewish Christians of the Early Centuries of Christianity According to a New Source*. Jerusalem: Central Press, 1966.

Portier-Young, Anathea. " Symbolic Resistance in the *Book of the Watchers*," in Angela Kim Harkins, Kelley Coblentz Bautch, and John C. Endres, eds., *The Watchers in Jewish and Christian Traditions*.Minneapolis: Fortress Press, 2014,

Porter, J. R. *The Lost Bible: Forgotten Scriptures Revealed*. New York: Shelter Harbor Press, 2010.

Porton, Gary G. *The Stranger within Your Gates: Converts and Conversion in Rabbinic Literature*, Chicago. The University of Chicago Press, 1994.

Pritz, Ray. *Nazarene Jewish Christianity*. Jerusalem: The Magnes Press, 1988.

Reed, Annette Yoshiko. *Fallen Angels and the History of Judaism and Christianity*. Cambridge: Cambridge Press, 2004.

Regev, Eyal. "Were the Early Christians Sectarians?" JBL 130, no. 4 (2011).

Roberts, A. and Donaldson, J. *The Ante-Nicene Fathers- the Clementina*. Grand Rapids: Wm. B. Eerdman's Publishing Company, 1978.

Roberts, A. and Donaldson, J, *The Ante-Nicene Fathers - Irenaeus-Volume I.* Grand Rapids: Wm. B. Eerdman's Publishing Company, 1978.

Rosenthal, Gilbert.S. "Jewish Attitudes Toward other Faiths: The Italian Model," Journal of Ecumenical Studies 44 (2009): 203-225.

Rowland, Christopher .*The Open Heaven: A Study of Apocalyptic in Judaism and Early Christianity.* New York: Crossroad, 1982.

Ruether, Rosemary. *Faith and Fratricide: The Theological Roots of Anti-Semitism.* New York: The Seabury Press, 1974.

Ruderman, David B. "A Jewish Apologetic Treatise from Sixteenth-Century Bologna," Hebrew Union College Annual Vol. 50 (1979): 253-276.

Runia, David T. *Philo In Early Christian Literature.* Minneapolis: Fortress Press, 1993.

Russel, D.S. *The Method and Message of Jewish Apocalyptic.* Philadelphia: Westminster, 1964.

Sherwin, Byron L. *Studies in Jewish Theology: Reflections in the Mirror of Tradition.* London: Valentine Mitchell, 2007.

Starret, Yehoshua. *The Breslov Haggadah.* New York: Breslov Research Institute, 1989.

Stern, Sacha. *Jewish Identity in Early Rabbinic Writings.* New York: Brill, 1994.

Saldarini, Anthony. *Matthew's Christian-Jewish Community.* Chicago: University of Chicago Press: 1994.

Saldarini, Anthony. *Pharisees, Scribes, and Sadducees in Palestinian Society*. Grand Rapids: Eerdmans, 1988.

Sanders, E.P. *Jewish and Christian Self-Definition in the Greco-Roman Period*. Philadelphia: Fortress, 1981.

Sanders, E.P. *Paul and Palestinian Judaism: A Comparison of Patterns of Religion*. London: SCM Press, 1977.

Sanders, Jack T. *Schismatics, Sectarians, Dissidents, Deviants*. Valley Forge: Trinity Press International, 1993.

Sarna, Nahum M. *The JPS Torah Commentary – Genesis*. Philadelphia: JPS: 1989.

Schaff, Philip. *The Nicene and Post- Nicene Fathers-Volume IV*. Grand Rapids: WM.B. Eerdmans Publishing Company, 1978.

Shanks, Hershel. *Ancient Israel: from Abraham to the Roman Destruction of the Temple*. Washington: BAS, 1999.

Sigal, Phillip. *The Halakhah of Jesus of Nazareth according to the Gospel of Matthew*. Atlanta: Studies in Biblical Literature, 2007.

Sim, David. *The Gospel of Matthew and Christian Judaism*. Edinburgh: T&T Clark, 1998.

Smelik, Klaas A.D. *Writings from Ancient Israel*. Louisville: Westminster, 1991.

Smith, Anthony D. *The Ethnic Revival*. Cambridge: Cambridge University Press, 1981.

Sparks, Kenton L. *Ethnicity and Identity in Ancient Israel*. Winona Lake: Eisenbrauns, 1998.

Schiffmann, Lawrence H. and Swartz, M. D. *Hebrew and Aramaic Incantation Texts from the Cairo Genizah*.Sheffield: Sheffield Academic Press, 1992.

Schiffman, Lawrence H. *The Eschatological Community of the Dead Sea Scrolls*. Atlanta: Scholars Press, 1989.

Schiffman, Lawrence H. *From Text to Tradition: A History of Second Temple and Rabbinic Judaism*. New York: Ktav, 1991.

Schiffman, Lawrence H. *Reclaiming the Dead Sea Scrolls: The History of Judaism, the Background of Christianity, the Lost Library of Qumran*. Philadelphia: JPS, 1994.

Schiffman, Lawrence H. *Who was a Jew?: Rabbinic and Halakhic Perspectives on the Jewish-Christian Schism*. KTAV: New York, 1985.

Schonfield, Hugh J. *According to the Hebrews*. London: Duckworth, 1937.

Schonfield, Hugh J .*The Pentecost Revolution*. New York: Elements, 1974.

Schonfield, Hugh J. *The History of Jewish Christianity*. London: Duckworth, 1936.

Shulvass, Moses A. *The History of the Jewish People*. Chicago: Regnery Gateway, 1982.

Simon, Marcel. *Versus Israel: A Study of the Relations between Christians and Jews in the Roman Empire (AD 135-425)*. Liverpool: Littman Library of Jewish Civilization, 1995.

Silva, Moises trans. *Esaias: A New English Translation of the Septuagint*. New York: Oxford University Press, 2009.

Skarsaune, Oskar *In the Shadow of the Temple.* Downers Grove: InterVarsity Press, 2002.

Staniforth, Maxwell *Early Christian Writings.* Middlesex: Penguin, 1968.

Stanton, Graham N. *Tolerance and Intolerance in Early Judaism and Christianity.* Cambridge: Cambridge University Press, 1998.

Stegmann, Ekkehard W. *The Jesus Movement: A Social History of Its First Century.* Minneapolis: Fortress Press,1999.

Strack, L. and Stemberger, Gunter. *Introduction to the Talmud and Midrash.* Minneapolis: Fortress Press, 1996.

Stevenson, J.*A New Eusebius.* London: S.P.C.K., 1957.

Stone Michael E. and Henze, Mattias.*4 Ezra and 2 Baruch: Translations, Introductions, and Notes.* Minneapolis: Fortress Press, 2013.

Studer, Basil. *Trinity and Incarnation: The Faith of the Early Church.* ed. Andrew Louth; trans. Matthias Westerhoff; Collegeville, Minn.: Liturgical Press, 1993.

Sullivan, Kevin. "The Watchers Traditions in *1 Enoch* 6-16: The Fall of Angels and the Rise of Demons," in Angela Kim Harkins, Kelley Coblentz Bautch, and John C. Endres, eds., *The Watchers in Jewish and Christian Traditions.* Minneapolis: Fortress Press, 2014.

Sumney, Jerry L. "Paul and Christ-Believing Jews Whom He Opposes," in *Jewish Christianity Reconsidered: Rethinking Ancient Groups and Texts*, ed. Matt Jackson-McCabe. Minneapolis: Fortress Press, 2007.

Swidler, Leonard "The Jewishness of Jesus: Some Religious Implications for Christians," Journal of Ecumenical Studies 18:1 Winter (1981): 104-113.

Talmon, Shemaryahu *Jewish Civilization in the Hellenistic-Roman Period.* Philadelphia, Trinity Press International, 1991.

Taylor, Joan E. *The Phenomenon of Early Jewish-Christianity: Reality or Scholarly Invention?* Vigiliae Christianae. Leiden: Brill, 1990.

Taylor, Joan E. *The Immerser: John the Baptist within Second Temple Judaism.* Grand Rapids: Eerdmans, 1997.

Tomson, Peter J. *Paul and the Jewish Law.* Minneapolis: Fortress, 1989.

Trachtenberg, Joshua. *The Devil and the Jews: The Medieval Conception of the Jew and Its Relation to Modern Anti-Semitism.* New Haven: Yale University Press, 1943.

Vanderkam, James C. *Enoch: A Man for All Generations.* Columbia: University of South Carolina, 1995.

Vermes, Geza. *Jesus the Jew.* Philadelphia: Fortress Press, 1981.

Vermes, Geza. *The Dead Sea Scrolls in English.* New York: Penguin, 1962.

Vermes, Geza. *The Complete Dead Sea Scrolls in English.* New York: Allen Lane, 1997.

Whiston, William. *The Works of Josephus.* Peabody: Hendrickson, 1987.

Wilson, Marvin R. *Exploring Our Hebraic Heritage: A Christian Theology of Roots and Renewal.* Grand Rapids: Wm. B. Eerdmans, 2014.

Wilson, Stephen G. *Related Strangers: Jews and Christians.* Minneapolis: Fortress, 1995.

Wise, Michael. *The Dead Sea Scrolls*. San Francisco: HarperCollins, 1996.

Williams, Lukyn *Adversus Judaeos: A Bird's Eye View of Christian Apologiae until the Renaissance*. Cambridge: Cambridge University Press, 1935.

Wolf, Hebert. *An Introduction to the Old Testament Pentateuch*. Chicago: Moody Press, 1991.

Wright, N.T. *Jesus and the Victory of God*. Minneapolis: Fortress Press, 1996.

Yonge, C.D. *The Works of Philo*. Peabody: Hendrickson, 1993.

Zeitlin, Irving. *Jesus and the Judaism of His Times*. New York: Polity Press, 1988.

Index

Abraham, 6
Adam, 6
Book of Parables, 133, 144, 146
Conversos, 223
Dead Sea Scrolls, 221, 226, 227, 233, 235, 236
Enoch, 1, 2, 6, 7, 8, 9, 10, 11, 13, 14, 15, 16, 17, 19, 20, 21, 22, 23, 24, 25, 26, 27, 28, 29, 30, 31, 32, 33, 34, 35, 36, 37, 38, 39, 40, 41, 42, 43, 44, 45, 46, 47, 48, 49, 50, 51, 52, 53, 55, 56, 57, 58, 59, 60, 61, 63, 64, 65, 66, 67, 68, 69, 70, 71, 73, 74, 75, 77, 78, 79, 80, 81, 82, 83, 85, 86, 87, 88, 89, 90, 91, 92, 93, 94, 95, 97, 98, 100, 102, 103, 104, 105, 106, 107, 108, 109, 110, 111, 112, 113, 114, 115, 116, 117, 118, 120, 121, 122, 123, 124, 125, 126, 127, 128, 129, 131, 132, 133, 134, 135, 136, 137, 138, 139, 140, 141, 142, 143, 144, 145, 147, 149, 150, 151, 152, 153, 154, 155, 156, 157, 158, 159, 160, 161, 163, 164, 165, 166, 167, 168, 169, 170, 171, 172, 173, 174, 175, 176, 177, 178, 179, 180, 181, 182, 183, 184, 185, 186, 187, 188, 189, 190, 191, 192, 193, 194, 196, 197, 198, 200, 201, 202, 203, 204, 205, 207, 209, 210, 211, 215, 216, 221, 229, 234, 235
Hellenism, 227
John Chrysostom, 230
Josephus, 235
Judaism, 156, 219, 220, 221, 224, 225, 227, 228, 229, 232, 233, 234, 235, 236
Judaisms, 134, 141, 143, 144, 145, 147, 150, 154, 155, 156, 223, 224, 225, 229
Memra, 220
Messiah, 15, 133, 134, 141, 143, 144, 145, 147, 150, 154, 155, 156, 225, 229
Mishnah, 222
Sadducees, 232
Similitudes of Enoch, 133
Son of Man, 133, 146, 148, 154, 156
Talmud, 100
Wisdom of Solomon, 154, 155, 156
Zealots, 220, 225

ABOUT THE AUTHOR

Juan Marcos Bejarano Gutierrez is a graduate of the University of Texas at Dallas. He earned a bachelor of science in electrical engineering. He works full time as an engineer but has devoted much of his time to Jewish studies. He studied at the Siegal College of Judaic Studies in Cleveland. He received a Master of Arts Degree in Judaic Studies. He completed his doctoral studies at the Spertus Institute in Chicago in 2015. He studied at the American Seminary for Contemporary Judaism and received rabbinic ordination in 2011 from Yeshiva Mesilat Yesharim.

Juan Marcos Bejarano Gutierrez was a board member of the Society for Crypto-Judaic Studies from 2011-2013. He has published various articles in HaLapid, The Journal for Spanish, Portuguese, and Italian Crypto-Jews, and Apuntes-Theological Reflections from a Hispanic-Latino Context, and is the author of *What is Kosher?* and *What is Jewish Prayer?* and *Secret Jews: The Complex Identity of Crypto-Jews and Crypto-Judaism*. He is currently the director of the B'nai Anusim Center for Education at CryptoJewishEducation.com, which provides additional information on the Inquisition and the phenomena of Crypto-Judaism.

Made in the USA
Coppell, TX
18 February 2021